THE LAZY COOK'S
FAMILY FAVOURITES

MO SMITH

First published in Great Britain in 2010 by
Allison & Busby Limited
13 Charlotte Mews
London W1T 4EJ
www.allisonandbusby.com

A CIP catalogue record for this book is available from
the British Library.

10 9 8 7 6 5 4 3 2 1

13-ISBN 978-0-7490-0782-9

Typeset by
Allison & Busby Ltd.

Paper used in this publication is from sustainably managed sources.
All of the wood used is procured from legal sources and is fully traceable.
The producing mill uses schemes such as ISO 14001
to monitor environmental impact.

Printed and bound in the UK by
CPI Mackays, Chatham ME5 8TD

THE LAZY COOK'S
FAMILY FAVOURITES

Mo Smith has been passionate about food since she was a young girl, when she used to help out in her father's grocery shop during the food rationing of the Second World War. Her philosophy has always been to promote fresh, seasonal ingredients and create healthy meals at speed. As well as cooking, she enjoys gardening, choral singing, public speaking and dress-making. She lives in a village in the Cotswolds, where she cares for her husband.

CONTENTS

FOREWORD

After many years of cooking and creating recipes, many of which I demonstrated to members of the public in my Cotswold kitchen, life suddenly changed when I became a carer for my husband. With extra household chores and a family of three teenagers to feed I had to rethink my style of cooking. I began by taking a fresh look at some of the ready-prepared ingredients available to me on the supermarket shelves and putting all my experience to the test by creating a completely new range of recipes. I called myself the 'Lazy Cook'.

Enjoying a weekend brunch is a relaxed way of entertaining friends or guests and the section headed *Breakfast & Brunch* recommends recipes to make the kitchen a relaxed place as well.

Everyone loves a party but being the host can be quite daunting so there's always the temptation to buy the canapés. But showing off your culinary skills to your friends needn't be stressful or difficult and in *Let's Party* I give you simple canapé recipes, which are prepared in advance so you can enjoy yourself and play the perfect hostess.

As well as recipes covering everyday cooking, you will find a section headed *From Plot to Pot*, recommending unusual ways of cooking your garden produce.

Cooking with children can be so much fun and is an important life skill for them to learn. In *Food for Hungry Tums*, you'll find a selection of easy recipes to cook with the kids. And for special treats, I've included some easy baking ideas in *Grandma, Can We Make Some Cakes?*

Whether you are a new mum keen to give baby healthy, home-cooked meals or a more experienced parent looking for some short cuts in the kitchen, *The Lazy Cook's Family Favourites* is for you. Using seasonal ingredients, these recipes are quick and easy to prepare and are ideally suited to the busy lifestyle of today's family.

If you have a wealth of experience of cooking or none at all, my Lazy Cook recipes will give novices confidence in the kitchen and new recipes and flavours for talented cooks to add to their repertoire. To make things even simpler for you, I've highlighted the recipes that are especially quick and easy to make with my Quick Fix star. There is also space for you to make your own comments on the 'Lazy Cook Notes' pages.
Armed with this book you are sure to impress not only yourself but your friends and family too.

Mo Smith
The Lazy Cook

BREAKFAST & BRUNCH

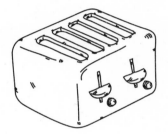

In most households a rushed weekday breakfast is limited to a quick bowl of cereal, bite of toast, or yoghurt. Many people have their breakfast standing up, on the way to work, or even worse, not at all. Thank heavens, then, for the weekend when there's more time to stretch this meal into the day and serve it as a more substantial brunch.

Any of the recipes in this section are suitable for early-bird breakfasters, as well as those who prefer to make a more leisurely start to their weekends. Saturdays and Sundays are for socialising so why not invite some friends round for brunch?

Read carefully through the recipes and note the ease with which they are prepared. You're sure to find something tasty to suit your guests.

BREAKFAST & BRUNCH

Scrambled Egg with Chives & a Curl of Smoked Ham

Herb Omelette

All-in-One Traditional English Breakfast

Breakfast Slices

Continental Platter of Cold Meats,
Fish and Cheese

Fresh Bread Rolls

Bread 'Offcuts'

Muesli

A Compote of Dried Fruits

Grilled Kippers

Kedgeree

Rice

Lamb Kidneys in a Devilled Cream Sauce

SCRAMBLED EGG WITH CHIVES & A CURL OF SMOKED HAM

So often, scrambled egg is served as a flavourless solid mass of overcooked ingredients, whereas the perfect scrambled egg should have a creamy texture and a delicious flavour. The key to success is to cook the ingredients over a medium heat, stirring continuously. I recommend that no more than 4 large eggs are scrambled at a time and preferably in a non-stick saucepan.

FOR EACH LARGE EGG USE:
50 ml (2 fl oz) of milk
7 g (¼ oz) of unsalted butter
Freshly ground black pepper
A few fresh chives (snipped with scissors)
1 wafer-thin slice of Black Forest or Parma ham

QUICK FIX

Gently heat the milk and butter in a pan until the butter has melted.

Add a little pepper, then crack a whole egg into the pan and immediately break the yolk using a wooden spoon or spatula.

Stir the ingredients continually until they form a soft, creamy texture, then remove from the heat.

Sprinkle in the chives, pile onto hot toast (there is no need to butter it) and serve with a curl of smoked ham on top.

LAZY COOK TIPS

Once the egg begins to cream together, the heat of the pan will continue the cooking process. At this point I recommend the pan is removed from the heat to avoid the egg overcooking and splitting – disaster! For easy cleaning, make sure you fill the saucepan with cold water as soon as the egg is removed.

HERB OMELETTE

BASIC INGREDIENTS FOR A 2 EGG OMELETTE:

12 g (½ oz) unsalted butter
2 large eggs
Freshly ground black pepper
A dessertspoon of chopped fresh parsley

Crack the eggs into a measuring jug, then add the chosen herbs and season. Using a fork, lightly whisk together – just a few turns is sufficient.

Heat a heavy-based (preferably non-stick) omelette pan over a high setting. Add the butter and, lifting the pan, swirl it around the base.

When hot, pour on the prepared eggs and immediately draw a wooden spatula through the eggs several times to build up layers of egg before they set.

Finally, tilt the pan to spread any remaining liquid egg. Fold in half and shake onto a hot serving plate.

Serve with bread and butter.

LAZY COOK TIPS

Omelettes must be cooked quickly (in seconds) over a high heat and a good pan is essential – preferably 15 cm (6 inches) in diameter. This should not be washed, but wiped with kitchen roll after each use and kept for omelette or crêpe/pancake making only. In addition to fresh herbs, grated cheese is another perfect filling for an omelette and should be added just before the omelette is folded. The heat of the omelette will melt the cheese to the perfect consistency. Other popular fillings are cooked ham or mushrooms – to be added before the omelette is folded. Not only is an omelette high in nutritional value, its speedy preparation means it's the perfect choice for breakfast.

All-in-One Traditional English Breakfast

To Prepare for a Crowd, for Each Serving:

1 tablespoon of olive oil
1 slice of bread (white or wholemeal)
1 large mushroom (wiped with damp kitchen roll)
1 medium egg
1 small tomato
A pinch of granulated sugar
2 rashers of back bacon or 4 lean streaky rashers

Set oven to gas mark 6/200°C/400°F/Aga roasting oven.

Heat the oil in a shallow roasting tin. Dip in the bread and leave dipped side down.

Remove the stalk from the mushroom and discard. Place the mushroom on top of the slice of bread, cavity facing upwards.

Crack an egg into the mushroom cavity, top with slices of tomato and sprinkle with a pinch of sugar.

Finally, top with the bacon slices and put into the preheated oven.

Cook for 10-15 minutes or until the bacon has cooked. Serve straight from the oven.

Lazy Cook Tips

The choice of mushroom is important: select one which will leave a cavity to hold the egg once the stalk is removed. An excellent way of serving breakfast or brunch to a crowd.

BREAKFAST SLICES

This recipe is ideal for serving at a brunch party and is also acceptable as a lunch or light supper.

Makes 6-8 slices
8 chipolata sausages
10 slices of rindless, lean streaky bacon
1 ring of black pudding (approximately 225 g/8 oz)
2 tablespoons of frozen spinach
8 large eggs

Cook the frozen spinach following the guidelines on the packet.

Place a large non-stick frying pan over a high heat and when hot add the bacon slices and the sausages. Reduce the heat slightly and cook, turning regularly. Remove them from the pan once they're done.

Take the black pudding and remove the skin before cutting it into thick slices. Add to the pan and brown quickly on each side before removing.

Using kitchen towel, mop up all excess fat from the pan, then toss in all the cooked ingredients and top with the cooked spinach. Whisk the eggs, then pour them over the mixture and cook until the egg begins to set and the base starts to brown.

Put under a grill (medium heat) or in an oven until the egg is set and the top begins to brown. Cut into slices and serve hot or cold.

LAZY COOK TIPS

For this recipe I use a 29 cm (11 inch) non-stick pan with a removable handle. The cooked bacon and sausages can be cut smaller (using scissors) as you return them to the pan mixing the flavours evenly. Frozen spinach is ideal for this recipe. Heat the grill before adding the egg to the pan ingredients, so that you're ready to complete the cooking. If cooking by Aga, heat the pan on the hot hob and transfer to the cooler hob once the ingredients are added. Then put into the roasting oven, towards the top, to complete the cooking.

Continental Platter of Cold Meats, Fish & Cheese

This can be a refreshing appetiser at breakfast and a welcome change from many of the hot foods that are so often on offer. There is a huge range of ingredients that can be included here: smoked ham and smoked salmon, a selection of salamis and continental sausages, and an assortment of cheese slices. The colours and the individual flavours do the work for you but as always, presentation is important. I would suggest arranging all the ingredients on a large platter or tray.
You may choose to add small bunches of grapes or seasonal fresh fruit to add a little sweetness and moisture. As a final touch and for eye-catching presentation, scatter with mustard cress immediately before serving. To complete this meal and make it into a memorable feast, serve your chosen platter with Bread 'Offcuts' (see p20) and/or Fresh Bread Rolls (see p18).

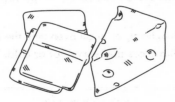

Serves a few or many

Arrange the following,
or ingredients of your choice, on a large platter:

Slices of cooked ham and salamis
Smoked salmon slices
An assortment of cheese slices

FRESH BREAD ROLLS

The advantage of this recipe is that the dough can be made in advance and kept in a fridge overnight, or for up to 2 days. When you're ready just shape and bake them, and savour that freshly baked bread aroma. Light and delicious, these are ideal for breakfast. Break them open while hot and drizzle with runny honey or maple syrup. Family and friends will be so impressed and I guarantee they will ask you for the recipe.

Makes 12
175 g (6 oz) of potatoes
450 g (1 lb) of plain white flour
50 g (2 oz) of unsalted butter
½ teaspoon of salt (optional)
20 g (¾ oz) of fresh yeast
1 teaspoon of granulated sugar
150 ml (5 fl oz) each of milk and water mixed together

Scrub the potatoes and remove any blemishes. Chop into small pieces and boil until soft.

Strain, discard the water, and allow the potatoes to cool a little.

Put the yeast and sugar into a measuring jug and top up to 300 ml (10 fl oz) with the mixture of milk and water. Stir well.

Chop the butter into small pieces, then combine with the flour, salt and the potatoes in a food processor.*

Blend for a few seconds, then pour in the yeast mixture until a ball of dough is formed.

Knead the dough for a few minutes, then place it in a large floured basin. Cover with a plate and transfer to the fridge.

After several hours the dough will have risen to the top of the basin. Push it down, turn it over and cut an 'x' on the top.

Cover again with the plate and return to the fridge.

Repeat this process as necessary until you are ready to shape and bake the rolls as follows.

Knead the dough a little before cutting into 12 pieces. Place these on a greased baking tray, sift with flour and put aside to rise.

Preheat the oven to gas mark 7/220°C /425°F/Aga roasting oven.

When the rolls have doubled in size, put them into the preheated oven and bake for 15-20 minutes.

To test if the rolls are cooked, tap them on the base. If they sound hollow, then they are ready.

Cool on a wire tray before serving.

*To mix by hand — Mash the cooked potatoes and put them into a large bowl with the flour, butter and salt and rub in with fingertips. Add the yeast mixture and work together by hand into a dough.

LAZY COOK TIPS

Although I sometimes use dried yeast for bread making, I have always only used fresh for this particular recipe.

Keep a tin of dried yeast in store and follow the instructions for using.

Bread 'Offcuts'

This recipe takes me right back to my childhood when my mother's friend visited and showed us how to make these rolls – she called them 'offcuts'. I can see them now rising in front of our open fire. The smell as they cooked was amazing and we ate them as though there was no tomorrow. I serve them for breakfast, sliced in half and toasted, topped with scrambled egg and a curl of smoked ham (see p13).

Makes 8-12
450 g (1 lb) of strong white flour
½ teaspoon of salt (optional)
50 g (2 oz) of unsalted butter (chopped into pieces)
25 g (1 oz) of fresh yeast
1 teaspoon of granulated sugar
300 ml (10 fl oz) of warm milk

Set oven to gas mark 7/220°C /425°F/Aga roasting oven (see Lazy Cook Tips).

Put the yeast and sugar into a measuring jug, add the milk and stir well.

In a food processor, blend the flour, salt and butter, then gently pour in the yeast mixture until a ball of dough is formed.

Lay the dough onto a lightly floured board or surface and knead until the texture is smooth and waxy. Shape into a round ball and cut into 4 pieces, then further divide these pieces into 2 or 3. Place each piece onto a lightly greased baking tray, spaced well apart, and press each down with the palm of your hand. Wait for them to rise until they double in size. Before placing in the preheated oven, press each down again with the palm of your hand. Bake for 15-20 minutes or until they are done (see Lazy Cook Tips).

Cool on a wire tray and serve immediately, or store in a polythene bag in the fridge or freezer for future use.

Lazy Cook Tips

The rolls are ready when they make a hollow sound when they are tapped on the base. I would recommend the oven is set halfway through the rising process.

MUESLI

For a delicious, healthy start to the day.

BASIC INGREDIENTS TO MAKE A LARGE BATCH:

1 kg (2 ¼ lbs) of jumbo oat flakes
225 g (8 oz) of sunflower seeds
450 g (1 lb) crimson or lexia raisins

Mix all the above ingredients together and store in an airtight container – I use a large, old-fashioned sweet jar.

To prepare a single portion for breakfast mix together:

50 g (2 oz) of the above basic mixture
1 teaspoon of sesame seeds
1 tablespoon of broad bran
2-3 walnut halves (broken into pieces)
A handful of dried cranberries
Pour over 2-3 fl oz of milk
Leave for 30 minutes, or longer, before eating.

LAZY COOK TIPS

Obviously, the choice of ingredients is yours. Fresh fruit can be added and in place of milk you can top it with plain or fruit yoghurt.

A Compote of Dried Fruits

I relish this simmering of dried fruits and serve it with breakfast cereals or my home-made Muesli (see p21). A packet of mixed dried fruits is an excellent store cupboard ingredient, especially during the autumn and winter months when many soft fruits are past their best.

QUICK FIX

Makes 8-10 helpings
450 g (1 lb) packet of mixed dried fruit halves
(apricots, prunes, pears, peaches)
1 carton of fresh orange juice
1 cinnamon stick

Set the oven to gas mark 3/160°C/325°F/Aga simmering oven.

Place the fruit in a casserole or ovenproof dish, with a lid.

Add the orange juice and cinnamon stick, cover, and bring to a simmer on a hob.

Transfer to the preheated oven and cook for 1 hour or until the fruits have softened.

Once cooled, cover and store in a fridge or cold larder.

Use within 4 days. Serve warm or cold.

Lazy Cook Tips

The fruits can be soaked in the orange juice for an hour or two before cooking to begin the softening process and shorten the cooking time.

Sweeten the cooked fruit with runny honey if the flavour is too tart for your palate.

This cooked fruit is also delicious served as a pudding with single cream.

GRILLED KIPPERS

Kippers are traditionally served for breakfast, but they also make a very appetising lunch. The preparation couldn't be quicker or easier: just put the grill on and wait a few minutes for them to heat up.

Allow one kipper per person.
Prepare and cook as follows.

Wipe each kipper with damp kitchen roll and place skin-side down in a grill pan or on a baking tray covered with lightly buttered tinfoil.

Smear a little butter over each kipper and grill at a medium-high temperature until the skin is dark brown and crisp.

Serve hot with bread and butter.

LAZY COOK TIPS

Buy kippers from a reputable fishmonger or a supermarket fish counter.

If cooking by Aga cook on the top runner of the roasting oven.

KEDGEREE

This is traditionally served in some households for breakfast on Boxing Day, but it makes an ideal dish to serve for brunch at any time of year.

Serve 6-8 breakfast portions
450 g (1 lb) of short-grain brown rice (boiled, see p25)
450 g (1 lb) of smoked haddock
1 large onion (skinned and finely chopped)
1 tablespoon of olive oil
4 large hard-boiled eggs (shelled and chopped)
Freshly ground black pepper
1 tablespoon of freshly chopped parsley
150 ml (5 fl oz) of single cream

Place the haddock in a pan of boiling water. Bring to a simmer and remove from heat, then cover and leave for 5 minutes.

Remove the haddock from the pan and break into flakes.

Discard the cooking water and wipe the pan dry with kitchen roll.

Heat the oil in a pan, add the prepared onions and cover.

Cook until they begin to soften, then add all the remaining ingredients, including the haddock, and stir well until hot throughout.

Serve hot or cold.

LAZY COOK TIPS

A cast-iron casserole dish is ideal for making kedgeree: it can then be served directly from the pan. You can make this with either brown or white rice, and butter can replace the cream. To speed up the process, the rice and eggs can be cooked a day or two in advance, stored in a fridge and used within 2 days.

Rice

To boil brown or white short grain:

Allow 50 g (2 oz) of rice per person.

Pour the grains into a sieve and rinse well under a cold tap.

Bring a large pan of water to the boil and add 1 teaspoon of salt (optional). Add the washed grains of rice and stir well.

Cover and simmer for 20 minutes or until cooked but with a nutty bite (see Lazy Cook Tips).

Strain into a sieve and rinse well under a cold running tap before serving.

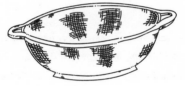

Lazy Cook Tips

The cooked grains should remain whole, tender and separate. If the rice is to be served hot, rinse after cooking in boiling water poured from a kettle.

The boiled rice can be stored, covered, in a fridge. Use within 2 days.

Serve cold from the fridge or reheat by rinsing in boiling water. Boiled rice is a most useful ingredient to have in store.

LAMB KIDNEYS IN A DEVILLED CREAM SAUCE

Serves 4 breakfast portions
8 lamb's kidneys
25 g (1 oz) of unsalted butter
150 ml (5 fl oz) of stock (meat or vegetable)
½ teaspoon of ready-made English mustard
1 tablespoon of Worcestershire sauce
1 tablespoon of single cream (optional)

Prepare the kidneys by cutting each in half and removing and discarding the centre core using scissors.

Heat a large non-stick frying pan over a high flame and when hot use a block of butter secured on a knife to grease the base. Add the prepared kidneys, cut-side down.

Reduce the flame slightly and cook for about 2 minutes on each side (or until they begin to brown) before removing from the pan. Add the stock, mustard and sauce to the pan and stir until simmering, scraping the residue from the base.

Return the cooked kidneys, cut-side down, and all the collected juices to the pan and bring to a simmer before stirring in the cream. Serve immediately in a heated dish or on toast.

LAZY COOK TIPS

A good butcher will sell the kidneys in their fat cases – all the better for storing and preservation of flavour. As the fat is removed and discarded a fine skin will remain which can easily be peeled away once the kidneys are cut in half. The pan juices from the cooked kidneys will be pink – this adds excellent flavour to the sauce. The kidneys may appear undercooked but the additional cooking in the simmering sauce will be sufficient and will preserve the delicate flavour.

LET'S PARTY

There is little I enjoy more than getting the family and friends together for a bit of a party! From the moment I greet them with either a glass of Pimm's on a summer's evening, or the aroma of hot punch as they enter my kitchen in winter, I am on a high.

Whether the invitation is for drinks and nibbles, or for a buffet-type meal, I make sure the food is simple but plentiful. For ease of eating, all canapés should be bite-sized, whilst a more substantial meal should be able to be served in soup bowls or dishes and eaten with a fork or spoon – enjoy!

LAZY COOK TIP

After-party essential: employ a youngster wanting to earn a little pocket money to do the washing up!

LET'S PARTY

Pastry Bases for Canapés

Wholemeal or Shortcrust Pastry

Ham & Stilton Bites

Olive & Apricot Relish

Anchovy & Sweet Tomato Relish

Chicken Liver Pâté

Fish Pâté

Cheese Savouries

In addition to the recipes listed above, I buy a selection of nuts and crisps.

Pastry Bases for Canapés

Makes 50
225 g (8 oz) shortcrust or wholemeal pastry (see p30)

Suggested toppings:

Chicken liver pâté (see p34) topped with a red or white seedless grape
Cream cheese seasoned with chopped parsley, topped with a piece of radish
Cream cheese topped with a curl of smoked salmon or Parma ham

To shape and bake the pastry bases:

Set oven to gas mark 6/200°C/400°F/Aga roasting oven.

Roll the pastry into a rectangle approximately 5mm (¼ inch) thick on a lightly floured surface, then put onto a lightly oiled baking tray.

Prick it all over with a fork before marking it into 3 cm (1 inch) squares and bake in the preheated oven for 10-15 minutes or until the pastry begins to change colour.

Remove from oven and snap or cut along the marked squares to separate.

Use immediately, or allow to cool before storing in an airtight tin or container until required.

Lazy Cook Tips

This method of shaping the bases is much quicker than using pastry cutters and transferring them one by one onto a baking tray.

When serving at a drinks party, bite-sized bases should be cut.

WHOLEMEAL OR SHORTCRUST PASTRY

100 g (4 oz) of plain white flour
100 g (4 oz) of wholemeal flour
100 g (4 oz) of lard (cut into pieces)
50-75 ml (2-3 fl oz) of cold water

Set oven to gas mark 6/200°C/400°F/Aga roasting oven.

In a food processor, blend the flours and lard together for a few seconds until they form a pastry crumb texture.

Keeping the machine switched on, pour the water in slowly until a ball of pastry is formed.

Shape into a ball and roll to the thickness required on a lightly floured board.

LAZY COOK TIPS

To make shortcrust pastry substitute the wholemeal flour with more all-white flour. Although we are often advised on the importance of allowing the pastry to rest in a fridge before baking, personally it's not something I adhere too. When I've tried this in the past, too often I've become distracted and forgotten all about it, ending up trying to roll rock-hard pastry. 'Keep it simple' is my motto. Make – roll – bake, then relax in anticipation of the result.

HAM & STILTON BITES

Prepare these little savouries in readiness to bake just before or during the party to wow your guests.

Makes 30
100 g (4 oz) of plain flour
50 g (2 oz) of cooked ham (torn into pieces)
50 g (2 oz) Stilton cheese (broken into pieces)
2 tablespoons of olive oil
1 teaspoon of wholegrain mustard
Freshly ground pepper
1 teaspoon of Worcestershire sauce
4 tablespoons of water

QUICK
FIX

Set the oven to gas mark 6/200°C/400°F/Aga roasting oven.

Blend the flour, ham and cheese together in a food processor.

Whisk the remaining ingredients together, then slowly add to the processed ingredients until a ball of paste is formed.

Drop teaspoons of the paste onto a lightly oiled baking tray and cook in the preheated oven for 10-15 minutes or until they begin to colour.

Serve warm.

LAZY COOK TIPS

These can be baked a few days before serving. Store in an airtight container and reheat to serve.

OLIVE & APRICOT RELISH

I created this relish from flavours I love. It presents a new and different taste to party canapés. This is a most unusual relish and as precious as caviar. It will intrigue your guests and you can have fun with them while they try to guess the ingredients.

QUICK
FIX

50 g (2 oz) of dried apricots
50 g (2 oz) of soft black pitted olives
½ teaspoon of dried thyme
1-2 tablespoons of Extra virgin olive oil

Process the apricots, olives and thyme together, then add enough oil to make a soft paste.

Store in jars and keep refrigerated. Use within 7 days.

To serve, spread a little paste onto small pastry bases (see p29).

Serve as canapés with drinks before a meal, or at a party.

LAZY COOK TIPS

It is essential to use the excellent flavour of 'soft' black pitted olives with a crinkly skin. These often come from Provence and are sold by weight, or from Spain and are sold in small packets.

ANCHOVY & SWEET TOMATO RELISH

Another Lazy Cook classic. This is quick and easy to make from everyday ingredients. It will add such interest to your meals, be they snacks, sauces or bite-sized savouries to serve with drinks.

75 g (3 oz) of fresh anchovy fillets
2 teaspoons of oil from the anchovies
4 heaped teaspoons of Italian tomato purée
2 teaspoons of runny honey

QUICK
FIX

Blend all the ingredients together to form a smooth paste.

Store in an airtight container and keep refrigerated. Use within 7 days.

To serve, spread onto bite-sized pieces of toast or small pastry bases (see p29) to serve as canapés with drinks before a meal or at a party.

OTHER USES FOR SERVING:

On breakfast toast
With cold salmon
On hard-boiled eggs (slice the egg in half and top with the relish)
Stirred into rice or pasta

LAZY COOK TIPS

It is essential to use fresh anchovies preserved in oil and sold by weight by a reputable fishmonger or supermarket fish counter.

Chicken Liver Pâté

Serves 4-6 as a starter

50 g (2 oz) of unsalted butter
1 shallot or small onion (skinned and finely chopped)
225 g (8 oz) of chicken livers
2 tablespoons of brandy
2 good pinches of dried herbes de Provence
Freshly ground white pepper
1 dried bay leaf
Extra butter for sealing

Melt half of the butter in a pan. When hot, add the shallot or onion and cook until it is soft. Remove, add a little more butter if necessary and melt, then add the chicken livers. Cook for approximately 2 minutes, turning them halfway through.

Transfer the livers and all juices into another bowl. Scrape all residue from the base of the pan, then add the brandy and boil for a few seconds.

Remove the pan from the heat and return the livers and juice, remaining butter and herbs, cooked shallot or onion, and season with pepper.

Allow it to cool slightly before putting into a food processor or liquidiser and blending to a smooth paste.

Pack into one big pot or small individual ones and press the bay leaf into the top.

If not needed for immediate use, melt approximately 50 g (2 oz) of butter and pour over the pâté to form a seal and, when set, store in a fridge.

Allow to return to room temperature before serving. Use within 7 days.

Lazy Cook Tips

This is excellent spread onto small pastry bases (see p29) and topped with a seedless grape to serve with party canapés. It is also good served with toast and salad for a light lunch or a starter to a meal.

FISH PÂTÉ

Rarely do I serve a more popular dish. This fish pâté is low in cost, simple to make and full of good, healthy ingredients. Hooray for tinned fish!

Serves 4

A small tin of either mackerel, sardine fillets or salmon, in olive oil
1 teaspoon of horseradish cream
1 teaspoon of Dijon mustard
1 teaspoon of cider vinegar
2 teaspoons of sun-dried tomato purée
4 anchovy fillets

Process or mash to a paste the chosen fish (including the oil or juices) with the remaining ingredients.

Serve in a dish or individual ramekins and top with a curl of anchovy.

Ideal served as a starter with toast, rolls or slices of bread flûte.

LAZY COOK TIPS

This pâté can be made in advance and stored, covered with cling film, in a fridge or cold larder. Serve within 3 days. Bring back to room temperature and top with curls of anchovy. Most tinned fish has excellent nutritional qualities and should be included in a weekly diet.

CHEESE SAVOURIES

These little balls made of cheese and butter and brandy - all the naughty things that should be resisted if you are attempting to shed a few pounds. But I say, why deprive yourself? Put the diet off until tomorrow!

Makes 40

50 g (2 oz) of breadcrumbs (fresh or dried, see p223)
1 tablespoon of freshly chopped parsley (or 1 teaspoon of dried)
1 small onion (skinned and finely chopped)
225 g (8 oz) of Stilton cheese (crumbled)
50 g (2 oz) of unsalted butter (softened)
1 tablespoon of brandy
1 teaspoon of Worcestershire sauce
Freshly ground white pepper

Mix half the breadcrumbs with all the parsley and put this mixture to one side.

In a food processor, blend together the remaining breadcrumbs and all other ingredients.

Drop teaspoons of the mixture onto the reserved breadcrumb and parsley mix; coat and shape into balls.

Serve immediately or store, in a covered container, in the fridge.

Bring back to room temperature before serving.

LAZY COOK TIPS

Stilton or any blue cheese can be used, or a mixture. This is a good recipe for using up all the leftover bits.

SOUPS

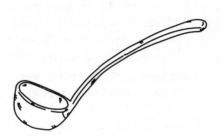

Served with crusty bread or rolls, soup will provide a nourishing meal at any time of the year. These days, with excellent vegetable stock cubes and modern food processors, as well as electric hand whisks that will purée ingredients without removing them from the cooking pot, making soup is quick and easy.

I recommend a large quantity is made for use over a few days. Store in a fridge or cold larder and heat the quantity required in a pan on a simmering hob.

Hot soups should be served hot but not piping hot and cold soups should be served icy cold.

SOUP RECIPES

Mushroom Soup

Pumpkin Soup

Bacon & Potato Soup

Celeriac & Sweet Potato Soup

Courgette & Orange Soup

Pea & Ham Soup

Parsnip & Watercress Soup

Lettuce Soup

And to accompany the soup:

Everyday Bread

Guidelines Applicable
to Soup Making

Make soup in advance, and once it's cooled, cover and store in a fridge or cold larder. Use within 4 days.

Reheat slowly to simmering point, stirring occasionally. Do not allow the soup to boil once cream has been added.

To soften vegetables:

I recommend softening onions and other vegetables in a little hot water. This will produce a few concentrated teaspoons of stock which will add goodness and flavour to your recipe without a trace of fat.

Soften in a little water only, with a lid on the pan. It takes 1-2 minutes depending on the amount of vegetables being softened.

Purée:

Use one of the modern electric hand whisks to purée the ingredients while in the pan. This avoids transferring them to a food processor or liquidiser – and the extra washing up!

Seasoning:

Use pepper, spices and herbs in place of salt.

Serving:

Present in individual bowls, a soup tureen or one large bowl. Serve with warm bread or rolls.

MUSHROOM SOUP

Serves 8-10
1 large onion (skinned and roughly chopped)
150 ml (5 fl oz) of milk
25 g (1 oz) of unsalted butter
2 teaspoons of mushroom ketchup
1 kg (2 lb 4 oz) of white cap mushrooms (wiped and roughly chopped)
900 ml (1½ pints) of vegetable stock
Freshly ground white pepper
2 tablespoons of single cream (optional)

Boil a little water in a large pan, add the prepared onion, cover and cook until softened.

Add the milk, butter, mushroom ketchup and mushrooms.

Cover the pan and simmer until the mushrooms have softened.

Using an electric hand whisk, purée the ingredients whilst in the pan.

Add all the remaining ingredients, then stir and simmer for 10 minutes before serving.

LAZY COOK TIPS

I find mushroom ketchup a most useful ingredient to keep in store. This quantity of mushrooms is packaged and sold in most supermarkets as 'Cooks' Ingredients'.

Pumpkin Soup

Serves 6-8
450 g (1 lb) of pumpkin flesh
225 g (8 oz) of potatoes (peeled and cut into small pieces)
2 large onions (skinned and roughly chopped)
1 litre (1¾ pints) of vegetable stock
230 g tin of chopped tomatoes in natural juices
Freshly ground black pepper
½ teaspoon of dried herbes de Provence
1 teaspoon of Dijon mustard
1 tablespoon of single cream
Several chives for garnish

Slice the pumpkin in half and remove the seeds and the pithy flesh in the centre.

Then skin the pumpkin, weigh the required amount and cut into small cubes.

Place all ingredients, except the cream and chives, into a large pan, and bring to a simmer.

Skim the top, then continue to simmer until the vegetables have softened (this can be done on a hob or in an Aga simmering oven and might take 30-45 minutes).

Using a slotted spoon, remove the solid ingredients and blend in a food processor until smooth.

Return to the pan, bring back to simmering and stir in the cream.

Garnish with a sprinkling of chives and serve.

Lazy Cook Tips

Pumpkin flesh absorbs a lot of liquid and a little more stock than may be necessary. The cooked ingredients can be pureed in the pan using an electric hand whisk. Pumpkin skin is very tough, take care when cutting.

BACON & POTATO SOUP

Serves 6
1 tablespoon of olive oil
1 large onion (skinned and chopped)
6 rashers of rindless streaky bacon (cut into small pieces)
900 g (2 lb) of potatoes (peeled and cut into small pieces)
1 small turnip (peeled and sliced thinly)
1 litre (1¾ pints) of vegetable stock
2 teaspoons of Dijon mustard
½ teaspoon of mixed dried herbs
Freshly grated nutmeg

Heat the oil in a large pan, then add the onion and bacon.

Stir and cook until beginning to soften, then add all the remaining ingredients and bring to a simmer.

Skim the top, then continue to simmer until the vegetables have softened (this can be done on a hob or in an Aga simmering oven and might take 30-45 minutes.

Using a slotted spoon, remove the solid ingredients and blend in a food processor until smooth.

Alternatively, puree the ingredients in the pan using an electric hand whisk.

Return to the pan and bring back to a simmer before serving.

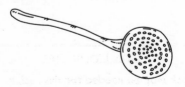

LAZY COOK TIPS

Home-made meat stock is ideal for this recipe.

CELERIAC & SWEET POTATO SOUP

Serves 6

1 large onion (skinned and chopped)
450 g (1 lb) of celeriac (peeled and chopped)
225 g (8 oz) of sweet potato (peeled and chopped)
600 ml (1 pint) of vegetable stock
1 teaspoon of fresh lemon juice
A handful of chopped fresh parsley (or a ½ teaspoon of dried)
2 tablespoons of single cream (optional)

Boil a little water in a large pan, add the prepared onion, cover and cook until softened.

Add the celeriac, sweet potato and half the stock and simmer, covered, for 10 minutes or until the vegetables have softened.

Using an electric hand whisk, purée the ingredients whilst in the pan.

Add all the remaining ingredients, stir and simmer for 10 minutes before serving.

LAZY COOK TIPS

A little more stock may be needed for this recipe.

Stir in at the end of the cooking and bring back to a simmer.

Store any remaining soup when cold, covered, in a fridge or cold larder and bring back to a simmer before serving.

Courgette & Orange Soup

Serves 4-6

1 medium onion (skinned and chopped)
500 g (1 lb) courgettes (washed, topped, tailed and sliced
6 fresh sage leaves (or several good pinches of dried)
600 m (1 pint) of chicken or vegetable stock
300ml (½ pt) of orange juice (from a carton)

Garnish

150 ml (¼ pint) of single cream (optional)
Grated zest of 1 fresh orange

Soften the onion in a covered pan of boiling water.

Add the prepared courgettes and the sage. Simmer, still covered, for 3-4 minutes to soften the courgettes.

Purée in a food processor, liquidiser or directly in the pan using an electric hand whisk.

Add the stock and orange juice and stir. Cover and simmer for 10 minutes.

Pour into a jug and when cold, cover and put into a refrigerator.

Serve from the refrigerator with a swirl of cream and grated orange zest on each portion.

Lazy Cook tips

This soup is delicious served cold. It will provide a refreshing start to a meal on a hot day. Use within 4 days.

PEA & HAM SOUP

Serves 4-6
1 large onion (skinned and chopped)
1 x 200 g packet of bacon lardons (chopped bacon)
900 ml (1 ½ pint) chicken stock
2 tablespoons of plain flour
A dash of milk
1 x 200 g tin of petits pois
1 handful of fresh mint (or 1 teaspoon of dried)
75 ml (2 oz) of single cream

Smear the base of a large pan with oil and when hot add the prepared onion and bacon lardons.

Stir and cook over a gentle heat, with the lid on the pan.

Add the flour to a little cold milk and mix to a smooth, runny paste.

Add the stock and the flour mixture to the pan and stir continuously over a gentle heat until it comes to the boil. Allow it to bubble like this for about a minute.

Add the petits pois and the mint. Bring to a simmer, place lid on pan and simmer for 5-10 minutes.

Allow to cool before storing overnight, covered, in a fridge.

Serve straight from the fridge. Stir in the cream and ladle into individual soup bowls.

LAZY COOK TIPS

This soup can also be served hot. Use within 4 days. I use a mixture of chicken and ham stock in this recipe.

The thickening with flour is optional. This is a quick soup to make and delicious served cold or hot. Make it with fresh garden mint, if available.

Parsnip & Watercress Soup

A hearty soup with a peppery flavour.

Serves 4

1 medium onion (peeled and chopped)
450 g (1lb) of parsnips (scrubbed, topped and tailed, and chopped)
600 ml (1 pint) of vegetable or chicken stock
1 bunch of fresh watercress
2 tablespoons of single cream

Soften the onion in a little boiling water with the lid on the pan. Add the prepared parsnips and 300 ml (10 fl oz) of water.

Simmer for 5-10 minutes or until the parsnips have softened.

Using a slotted spoon, remove the onion and parsnips, and blend in a liquidiser or processor.

Return the liquid to the pan, then add the stock. Cover and simmer for 10 minutes.

Roughly chop up the watercress, add to the pan and simmer for a few minutes. For presentation, stir in the cream and serve.

Lazy Cook Tips

Make this soup at the beginning of winter when parsnips and watercress are at their best.

Aga users should transfer the pan to the simmering oven for the final stage.

This is an excellent soup to make in advance and keep in the fridge until needed.

LETTUCE SOUP

Serve cold. Deliciously refreshing.

Serves 6-8
1 tablespoon of olive oil
4 thick rindless rashers of bacon (roughly chopped)
1 large onion (peeled and chopped)
2 good-sized lettuces (washed)
A good handful each of fresh mint and sage (or a ½ teaspoon of each dried)
2 tablespoons of fresh lemon juice
900 ml (1½ pints) of stock (ham if possible)
Freshly ground white pepper
150 ml (¼ pint) of single cream (optional)

Heat the oil in a large pan, add the bacon and onion, and then cook until softened.

Add the lettuce, herbs, lemon juice and about 150 ml (5 fl oz) of water.

Cover and simmer until the lettuce has reduced and wilted.

Using an electric hand whisk, purée the ingredients whilst in the pan.

Add all the remaining ingredients, stir and simmer for 10 minutes.

Allow to cool, then put in the fridge to chill further.

Serve from the fridge in a tureen or in individual soup bowls, with a swirl of cream poured on top.

LAZY COOK TIPS

Make this soup a day in advance if possible. Serve directly from the fridge. If ham stock is not available add salt to taste.

EVERYDAY BREAD

TO MAKE A 900G (2 LB) WHITE LOAF: (SEE BELOW FOR VARIATIONS):

450g (1 lb) of strong white bread flour
1 teaspoon of salt (optional)
15g (½ oz) of fresh yeast (see below if using dried yeast)
1 level teaspoon of granulated sugar
300 ml (10 fl oz) of warm water
1 generous tablespoon of olive oil

Lightly oil or grease a 900 g (2 lb) loaf tin.

Put the yeast and sugar into a measuring jug, add a little warm water and cream together.

Add the oil and enough warm water to make up to 300ml (10 fl oz).

Process the flour and salt together for a few seconds before pouring in the liquid yeast mixture, switch off as soon as a dough is formed.

Place the dough onto to a lightly floured surface and knead until it becomes smooth and waxy in texture (this should take about 2 minutes). Shape to fit the prepared loaf tin and sift the top with flour.

Leave to rise above the tin before placing it in the preheated oven (gas 7/220°C/425°F/Aga roasting oven) and bake for 25-30 minutes.

Remove the loaf from the tin and tap the base. If it sounds hollow, the loaf is baked. If not, return it to the oven for a further few minutes baking.

Allow the loaf to cool on a wire tray. Store in a polythene bag in the fridge and use within 7 days or freeze.

LAZY COOK TIPS

Buy dried active yeast for hand-baking and follow the directions on the tin to make up. Fresh yeast is usually available from a good baker. Store in the fridge and use within 5 days.

Everyday Bread variations

Light Wholemeal Loaf

I have at last 'weaned' my husband from white bread and I have done so by making a very light wholemeal loaf. I have to say it is very acceptable even to our 2-year-old grandson Charlie, who ate lots and even made his own little bread roll – get them baking young!

Instead of using 450g (1 lb) of strong white bread flour, use only 325 g (12 oz) and make up the remaining 125 g (5 oz) with strong wholemeal bread flour

Standard Wholemeal Loaf

Use half the quantity of strong white bread flour and half the quantity of strong wholemeal bread flour and slightly increase the amount of yeast liquid by adding an extra tablespoon of warm water.

100% Wholemeal Loaf

Use all strong wholemeal or granary bread flour and increase the amount of yeast liquid by adding an extra tablespoon of warm water. The optional addition of a dessertspoon of molasses or black treacle will add good flavour.

Lazy Cook tips

The warmth of the kitchen will be sufficient to rise the dough, the longer it takes to rise the better the resulting bread. With practice you will be able to judge when to set the oven in readiness for baking. The temperature can be reduced to gas 4/180°C/350°F/a lower shelf of an Aga, after the first 20 minutes of baking to avoid too brown a crust.

Lazy Cook Notes

STARTERS & LIGHT MEALS

Sharing a meal with the family and friends remains one of my greatest pleasures, but since I have become increasingly 'lazy' such entertaining has been pruned to absolute simplicity. Elaborate dinner parties are out, supper parties are in! As a result I have less work to do and the whole evening is far more relaxed.

This does not mean that I dislike starters. On the contrary, I enjoy them very much. And the best thing about them is that with a little effort they can be turned into a light meal.

Starters are usually served at the beginning of a meal and the content, colour and appearance should be such that they stimulate the appetite for things to come, whether it is a simple half grapefruit or a bowl of soup.

Under this heading you will find many recipes for starters, most of which, by increasing the portion size, can be transformed into an acceptable light meal. I find such recipes especially valuable at weekends when a rest from everyday cooking is welcome.

STARTERS & LIGHT MEALS

Cheese & Onion Flan

Cheesy Eggs

Warm Savoury Cheesecake with
a Goat's Cheese Topping

Classic Cheese Soufflé

Lazy Cheese Soufflé

Baked Avocado with Goat's Cheese

Baked Peach Halves with a Savoury Filling

Terrine

Poached Egg with a Rocket & Parma Ham Salad

Ox Tongue Rolls with Prawns & Mustard Mayonnaise

Herring Roes with a Black Butter Sauce

Dessert Pear with Smoked Salmon
& Peppered Cream Sauce

Mussels Wrapped in Bacon served on a Bed of Noodles
with a Marmalade Pickle

Mediterranean Tart

Pepper Cups Filled with an Anchovy Paste
and a Last-Minute Sauce

Beef Tomatoes with a Savoury Filling

Open Sandwiches

Fresh Figs in Little Bread Baskets

Smoked Salmon & Prawn Parcels
with a Peppered Cream Sauce

CHEESE & ONION FLAN

Serves 6 slices
20 cm (8 inch) ready-baked savoury pastry case
1 large onion (skinned and sliced)
100 g (4 oz) of Stilton cheese
2 large eggs
300 ml (10 fl oz) of whole milk
Freshly ground black pepper

QUICK
FIX

Set the oven to gas mark 4/180°C/350°F/Aga baking oven.

Soften the onion in a covered pan in just a little boiling water.

Place the pastry case on a baking tray and cover the base with the cooked onion, strained from the pan juices.

Grate the cheese over the top and season with freshly ground black pepper.

Add the milk to the pan juices and warm.

Whisk the eggs in a bowl, then add the warmed milk and whisk again before pouring through a sieve onto the pastry case ingredients.

Cook in the preheated oven for 20-30 minutes, or until set and beginning to brown slightly on top.

Serve warm or cold with salad.

LAZY COOK TIPS

Every household should have these simple ingredients in store at all times. A ready-baked pastry case is a lifesaver. Savoury and sweet ready-baked pastry cases are available from most delicatessens and supermarkets. This flan is made in minutes and the result is stunning. It's also a good recipe for using up odd ends of cheese.

CHEESY EGGS

Serves 4-6
6 medium eggs (hard-boiled)
25 g (1 oz) of butter
25 g (1 oz) of plain flour
600 ml (1 pint) of milk
100 g (4 oz) of Gruyère cheese (grated)
2 tablespoons of single cream
Fresh chives (snipped with scissors)
Freshly ground white pepper

Set the oven to gas mark 6/200°C/400°F/Aga roasting oven.

Shell and slice the eggs and arrange them over the base of a shallow ovenproof dish.

Melt the butter in a pan, stir in the flour and cook over a gentle heat until it blends into a smooth paste.

Add the milk and continue stirring until the sauce boils and thickens.

Remove from the heat, stir in the cheese, cream, chives and pepper, and pour over the eggs.

Bake in the preheated oven (or under a grill) until it is hot and bubbly before serving.

LAZY COOK TIPS

Should the sauce become lumpy, remove it from the heat and whisk until smooth before continuing to cook. This recipe can be prepared in individual ramekins. Serve as a starter or as a light meal. Prepare in advance and store (covered) in a fridge or cold larder.

WARM SAVOURY CHEESECAKE WITH A GOAT'S CHEESE TOPPING

This is an unusual cheesecake; it is light in texture and so tasty.

Serves 6-8 slices
100 g (4 oz) of plain flour
1 teaspoon of baking powder
1 teaspoon of caster sugar
3 large eggs
100 g (4 oz) of full fat cream cheese
1 jar of sun-dried tomatoes in olive oil
50 g (2 oz) of pitted black olives
Freshly ground white pepper
350 g (10 oz) of goat's cheese

Set the oven to gas mark 4/180°C/350°F/Aga baking oven.

Put a parchment paper case into an 18 cm (7 inch) round cake tin with a loose base.

In a food processor, mix the flour, baking powder, sugar, eggs and cream cheese together to make a smooth paste.

Now add 6 sun-dried tomatoes, the olives and pepper and process for a few seconds only.

Pour into the prepared tin and bake for 25-30 minutes or until set.

Allow to cool a little before scattering with a few sun-dried tomatoes and covering with goat's cheese slices.

Return to the oven for a couple of minutes until the goat's cheese has melted. Allow to cool before removing from the tin. Peel off the paper case and slice to serve.

LAZY COOK TIPS

As an alternative presentation bake the cake and, when cold, spread the top with a good layer of curd or cream cheese with lots of freshly chopped parsley added. Garnish with radish flowers, spring onions and other salad ingredients of your choice.

CLASSIC CHEESE SOUFFLÉ

*Hot soufflés are amongst the most neglected of savoury dishes.
There is a myth about them which implies they can only be produced
by top chefs in expensive restaurants. This is not so. They are really
very simple to prepare and bake. Read through my Lazy Cook Tips
and you will find this and other soufflé recipes so easy to cook. Your
family and friends will love them.*

Serves 4-6
25 g (1 oz) of unsalted butter
12 g (½ oz) of plain flour
150 ml (5 fl oz) of whole milk
3 egg yolks
4 egg whites
A few pinches of mustard powder
A few pinches of cayenne pepper
50 g (2 oz) of mature Stilton (grated)
50 g (2 oz) of Gruyère (grated)
A little grated Parmesan for a final garnish

Set the oven to gas mark 4/180°C/350°F/Aga baking oven.

Butter well the base and sides of one large (size 2) porcelain soufflé dish.

Tie a piece of buttered greaseproof paper around the outside to project
about 5 cm (2 inches) above the rim and secure the ends with a paper clip.

Stand the prepared dish on a baking tray.

Melt the butter in a pan large enough to take all the ingredients.

Remove it from the heat before the butter becomes too hot and stir in the
flour until it is of a smooth consistency (this is called a roux).

Stir in the milk and return to a gentle heat. Stir continuously until it thickens,
then remove from the heat and allow it to cool for just a few minutes before
beating in the egg yolks and several good pinches each of mustard powder
and cayenne pepper.

Whisk the egg whites until they peak, then add one tablespoon of egg white to the roux. Mix in the cheeses too.

Carefully fold in the remaining egg white and pour into the prepared dish.

Transfer immediately to the preheated oven and bake for 20-30 minutes or until it has risen and set.

Remove the paper and sprinkle with grated Parmesan. Serve straight from the oven.

LAZY COOK TIPS

The secrets of success here are to have all of the ingredients to hand, the cheeses grated, the oven up to temperature and the dish prepared before beginning to make the soufflé.

I recommend the butter is melted but not hot before the flour is added; this will ensure a smooth paste (roux).

Soufflés rise from below and, if you cook by Aga, place it on the floor of the baking oven.

Cook in the centre of a gas or fan heated oven, placing it on a preheated baking tray.

I like soufflés crisp on the outside and spongy in the middle – test by piercing the centre with a metal skewer, preferably warm.

Bring the guests to the table a few minutes before the soufflé is baked and carry it to the table on a hot serving plate.

Test this one on the family so that you know exactly how long it will take to bake!

LAZY CHEESE SOUFFLÉ

If you doubt your culinary skills will extend to tackling the classic soufflé I feel sure you will be able to handle this simplified version which is just as delicious.

Serves 4
6 slices of bread (brown or white)
225 g (8 oz) of grated cheese
425 ml (15 fl oz) of whole milk
3 large eggs
Freshly ground white pepper
2 teaspoons of Dijon mustard
1 teaspoon of anchovy essence

Set the oven to gas mark 4/180°C/350°F/Aga baking oven.

Layer the bread and cheese into a soufflé or pie dish, beginning and ending with bread.

In a measuring jug, whisk the eggs, add the mustard and anchovy essence and season with pepper.

Warm the milk, then add it to the eggs and whisk together.

Pour through a sieve over the layered bread and leave for 15-20 minutes.

Stand the dish on a baking tray and bake in the preheated oven for 30-40 minutes, or until risen.

Serve straight from the oven as a starter, or with peas, mangetout, or salad as a light meal.

LAZY COOK TIPS

This is a good recipe for using up ends of cheese, especially Stilton which will give excellent flavour.

It can be prepared and left for a longer period before baking if it suits your time plan.

BAKED AVOCADO WITH GOAT'S CHEESE

Avocados are usually sliced and served cold. Cooking them with additional ingredients, as in this recipe, turns them into an unusual and nutritious light meal.

Serves 4
2 avocados
4 teaspoons of apple purée
4 slices of goat's cheese

QUICK FIX

Set oven to gas mark 6/200°C/400°F/Aga roasting oven.

Slice each avocado in half lengthways and remove and discard the centre stone.

Fill each cavity with apple purée and top with a slice of goat's cheese.

Transfer to a shallow ovenproof dish or metal tray and bake in the preheated oven for 10-15 minutes, or until the cheese has melted.

Serve hot from the oven with salad and fresh rolls.

LAZY COOK TIPS

Slice a little flesh from the base of each avocado half so that they will stand firm while cooking.

If the avocado is a little unripe baking will soften it. They can also be cooked under a grill.

You can use shop-bought apple purée or prepare your own (see p215).

Use small avocados if serving as a starter.

Baked Peach Halves with a Savoury Filling

A refreshing snack on a hot summer's day.

Serves 1 or many

For each ripe peach you need:
1 teaspoon of wholegrain mustard
2 thin slices of goat's cheese
2 slices of Parma ham
A small handful of watercress
1 whole radish
Olive oil
Balsamic vinegar

Set the oven to gas mark 4/180°C/350°F/Aga baking oven.

Slice the washed peach in half, then remove and discard the stone.

Fill the cavities with a little wholegrain mustard and top with a slice of goat's cheese and a crumpled slice of Parma ham.

Place on a baking tray or in an ovenproof dish and bake for 5-10 minutes in the preheated oven.

Serve with a few sprigs of watercress topped with a whole radish and drizzled with oil and balsamic vinegar (one-third vinegar to oil).

Serve hot or cold, allowing one half of a peach per person as a starter, or two halves as a light snack with toasted brioche.

Lazy Cook Tips

Cut a sliver of flesh from the base of the peach halves so that they will stand firm while cooking. I recommend Moutarde de Meaux 'Pommery' wholegrain mustard.

A little hot water can be added to the dish to encourage softening of the peaches during cooking.

TERRINE

A terrine is one of those really useful standbys, especially for unexpected visitors when suddenly a snack round the kitchen table seems like a nice idea.

Serves 8
225 g (8 oz) of lamb's liver
450 g (1 lb) of pork belly (rind removed)
6 venison (or gamey) sausages (skin removed)
50 ml (2 fl oz) of red wine
Freshly ground black pepper
Several good pinches of mixed dried herbs
Bay leaves

Cut the liver and pork into approximately 3 cm (1 inch) cubes.

Mix all of the ingredients together (except the bay leaves) and leave to marinate for 2 hours, stirring occasionally.

Pack the mixture into one large, or several smaller pots, top with a bay leaf, and then cover.

Stand the pots in a pan or roasting tin containing enough warm water to come halfway up the pots.

Place in a preset oven (gas mark 3/160°C/325°F/Aga simmering oven) and cook for 1-1½ hours, or until the centre is firm to the touch and the ingredients are shrinking slightly from the sides of the pot.

Remove from the oven and, once cooled, cover and store in a fridge or cold larder. Return to room temperature before serving. Eat within 5 days.

LAZY COOK TIPS

Special pots with lids are available, but if you do not have these then the terrine can be cooked in any ovenproof dish, and covered with foil secured with string. Although the recipe suggests marinating for 2 hours, this can be extended to overnight. Stir the ingredients before packing into the pots for cooking. Serve with toast and watercress.

Poached Egg with a Rocket & Parma Ham Salad

QUICK FIX

To make individual servings:

1 egg

1 teaspoon of vinegar

1 thick slice of bread or brioche (toasted)

Butter (optional)

Rocket (washed and dried)

1 pickled gherkin or cornichon (sliced)

Vinaigrette (see p185)

1 slice of Parma or Black Forest smoked ham

Freshly ground black pepper

A sprinkling of chives

To poach the eggs pour approximately 300 ml (10 fl oz) of water into a small pan and add a few drops of vinegar.

When this comes to the boil, crack an egg into it, cover, and simmer gently for 2-3 minutes, or until the egg is cooked to your liking.

Meanwhile, make and butter the toast and lay it on a serving plate.

Garnish with the prepared rocket, then add the slices of gherkin and a spoonful of vinaigrette.

Finally, top with a slice of crumpled ham.

Lay the poached egg on top, season with freshly ground black pepper and garnish with a sprinkle of cut chives.

Serve immediately.

Lazy Cook Tips

Whisk the boiling water before adding the egg for an even coagulation. Watercress can be used in place of rocket.

This makes for a light but substantial lunch.

Ox Tongue Rolls with Prawns & Mustard Mayonnaise

Serves 4
4 slices of ox tongue
100 g (4 oz) of Le Roulé cream cheese with herbs
A little milk
Freshly ground white pepper
1 lemon
100 g (4 oz) of cooked prawns
Watercress
Mayonnaise (home-made or bought – see p185)
English mustard
Cocktail sticks

Soften the cheese with a little milk and season with pepper and lemon juice.

Spread the mixture over the tongue slices, top with prawns, roll up and secure with a cocktail stick.

Place on individual plates or on one serving platter and garnish with watercress.

Serve with mayonnaise seasoned with ready-made mustard, alongside buttered toast or thick bread slices.

Lazy Cook Tips

Ox tongue is, I think, a neglected ingredient. The flavour and texture is delicate and delicious; this is just one of the ways in which I present it.

HERRING ROES WITH A BLACK BUTTER SAUCE

Serve on a bed of salad leaves.

Serves 4

225 g (8 oz) of herring roes (washed and dried on kitchen roll)

A little flour seasoned with freshly ground pepper

50 g (2 oz) of butter

A splash of balsamic vinegar

Mixed salad leaves

Freshly chopped parsley

QUICK
FIX

Melt half the butter in a non-stick frying or sauté pan.

Lightly coat the roes in seasoned flour and cook in the butter until brown and firm to the touch (approximately 3 minutes on each side).

Remove from pan and keep warm.

Add the remaining butter to the pan juices and, when melted and changing colour, add the balsamic vinegar and stir before removing from heat.

Place the cooked roes on a bed of mixed salad leaves set on individual plates.

Pour the sauce over the roes and garnish with freshly chopped parsley.

Serve with brown bread and butter.

LAZY COOK TIPS

Herring roes are a most neglected ingredient. They are inexpensive and available throughout the winter months.

Quick and easy to prepare, they have a unique flavour and texture.

DESSERT PEAR WITH SMOKED SALMON & PEPPERED CREAM SAUCE

The combination of these flavours is so light and refreshing.

Serves 4

2 dessert pears

1 x 80 g packet of Boursin peppered cheese

225 g (8 oz) of smoked salmon

4 fresh anchovy fillets

4 thin slices of fresh lemon

Fresh parsley sprigs

4 thin slices of brown bread (buttered and cut into quarters)

QUICK FIX

Cut the pears in half lengthways, then remove the stalk and centre pith and skin them.

Fill each cavity with peppered Boursin and place, cut-side down, onto individual plates.

Cover each pear with strips of smoked salmon. Top with a curled anchovy fillet.

Garnish the tip of the pears with a lemon slice and a sprig of fresh parsley.

Heat the remaining Boursin with a little milk to make a runny sauce which can be trailed round each pear.

Serve with brown bread and butter.

LAZY COOK TIPS

Very quick to prepare and eye-catching in presentation, this is an excellent starter or light lunch or supper recipe.

Fresh anchovy fillets can be purchased from most delicatessens or supermarkets and I recommend these in preference to tinned or bottled. I have used both Comice and Conference pears in this recipe.

Mussels Wrapped in Bacon served on a Bed of Noodles with a Marmalade Pickle

Serves 4
12 large cooked mussels
6 rashers of rindless streaky bacon
2 shallots (skinned and finely chopped)
Cooked egg noodles
Marmalade Pickle (see below)

Set the oven to gas mark 6/200°C/400°F/Aga roasting oven.

Wrap each mussel in half a rasher of streaky bacon, put on a skewer and place in a baking tin and bake for 10-15 minutes, turning halfway through.

To serve in individual portions, place some of the cooked noodles in the centre of 4 hot serving dishes, top each with three mussel rolls and pour a little of the marmalade pickle over. Serve any remaining pickle separately.

Marmalade Pickle

2 shallots (skinned and finely chopped)
2 teaspoons of wine vinegar
2 tablespoons of orange marmalade
Freshly ground pepper
A good pinch of ground cloves

Soften the shallots in a little boiling water, with the lid on the pan.

Stir in the marmalade, vinegar, pepper and ground cloves, and bring to a simmer. Taste and add a little more wine vinegar to sharpen the flavour if necessary.

Lazy Cook Tips
Cook the rolls under a grill if it is more convenient.

MEDITERRANEAN TART

Serves 6

20 cm (8 inch) ready-baked savoury pastry case
1 large red onion (skinned and sliced)
1 280g jar of sun-dried tomatoes preserved in oil
75 g (3 oz) of pitted dry black olives
2 large eggs
300 ml (10 fl oz) of whole milk
Freshly ground black pepper
Handful of chopped fresh oregano (or 1 teaspoon of dried)

QUICK
FIX

Set the oven to gas mark 4/180°C/350°F/Aga baking oven.

Soften the onion in a covered pan in just a little boiling water.

Place the pastry case on a baking tray and cover the base with the cooked onion, strained from the cooking liquid.

Cover with sun-dried tomatoes and toss in the olives. Season with freshly ground black pepper.

Pour the milk into the pan with the pan juices and warm. Whisk the eggs in a jug, then add the warmed milk and whisk again before pouring through a sieve onto the pastry case ingredients.

Sprinkle oregano over the top and cook in the preheated oven for 20-30 minutes, or until set and beginning to brown slightly on top.

Serve it warm or cold with salad.

LAZY COOK TIPS

This flan is bursting with colour and flavours and with all the ingredients in general store, including the ready-baked pastry case, it is made in minutes. I prefer the flavour of soft pitted olives (they have wrinkled skins). They are often sold by weight or in packets.

Savoury and sweet ready-baked pastry cases are available from most delicatessens and supermarkets — I panic if I don't have a couple or more in my store cupboard.

Pepper Cups Filled with an Anchovy Paste and a Last-Minute Sauce

Serves 4

Main ingredients:

2 large peppers
1 tablespoon of olive oil

Filling:

25 g (1 oz) of brown breadcrumbs (see p223)
25 g (1 oz) of cooked ham or bacon
6 anchovy fillets
4 pitted black olives
2 sun-dried tomatoes
1 teaspoon of green olive pesto
1 teaspoon of olive oil
Freshly ground black pepper
1 tablespoon of fresh parsley (chopped)
1 tomato
A few shavings of butter

Sauce:

5 fl oz (150 ml) of vegetable stock or hot water
Tomato ketchup

Set the oven to gas mark 6/200°C/400°F/Aga roasting oven.

Cut the peppers in half leaving each with a little of the green stalk. Remove the seeds and fleshy bits.

Place the peppers cut-side down in a lightly oiled roasting tin or ovenproof dish.

Brush with oil and bake in the preheated oven until the skins begin to soften and brown (10-15 minutes).

Reserving a little of the parsley, the tomato and the butter, blend all of the remaining filling ingredients in a food processor until they make a sticky paste.

Fill each cooked half pepper with the paste, top with a slice of tomato, a dot of butter and a sprinkling of fresh parsley.

Return to the oven for 5-10 minutes to cook the tomato and heat the filling.

Serve with a little salad garnish and Last-Minute Sauce.

LAST-MINUTE SAUCE

Pour 5 fl oz (150ml) of hot water (or vegetable stock) into the roasting tin in which the peppers have been baked.

Whisk in a couple of shakes of tomato ketchup, bring to the boil and serve.

LAZY COOK TIPS

I recommend anchovy fillets preserved in oil; these are now available from most delicatessen counters.

If catering for a crowd choose peppers of assorted colours — they look really good presented on a large serving platter. This is a recipe with excellent flavours.

BEEF TOMATOES WITH A SAVOURY FILLING

Makes 4

4 beef tomatoes

4 heaped tablespoons of breadcrumbs

4 spring onions (thinly sliced)

12-16 anchovy fillets (cut into small pieces)

Fresh mint (roughly chopped)

Freshly ground black pepper

1 teaspoon of runny honey

Set the oven to gas mark 6/200°C/400°F/Aga roasting oven.

Chop off the top (stalk end) of the tomatoes and set aside for now.

Remove the pips and centre core and put these into a sieve placed over a basin to collect all the juices.

Add the remaining filling ingredients to the juices and stir together. Discard the core and pips.

Stuff the mixture into the prepared tomatoes, and cover with the reserved tops. Place in a lightly oiled, shallow, ovenproof dish. Brush each tomato lightly with oil and bake in the preheated oven for 15-20 minutes. Serve hot, warm or cold.

Serve with salad for a delicious light lunch. If you are presenting these as a starter, use smaller tomatoes. They can also be served as a vegetable accompaniment to cooked meat or fish.

LAZY COOK TIPS

Use a grapefruit knife to remove the centre core and pips from the tomatoes. The filling should be of a moist consistency; add a little stock or warm water if it is too dry. Make breadcrumbs in a blender or processor or use dried breadcrumbs (see p223). This dish can also be cooked on a barbecue; just wrap them individually in foil before cooking.

Open Sandwiches

There is something so eye-catching about open sandwiches and the toppings can be varied and plentiful.

Serves 1 or a crowd
For each person you will need:
1 medium slice of wholemeal bread (crusts removed)
Cream cheese seasoned with fresh parsley (chopped)
Several slices of cucumber (skin removed)
Slices of radish
A few seedless red grapes
3-4 wafer-thin slices of Black Forest smoked ham
1 soft boiled egg – shelled
Mustard cress
Mayonnaise (see p185)

Spread each bread slice liberally with the prepared cheese. Top with cucumber slices, radish and grapes and the ham slices. Finally top with shelled egg and sprinkle with mustard cress. Serve with mayonnaise, home-made (see p185) or bought.

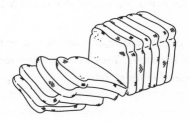

LAZY COOK TIPS

I find this presentation is really popular and I have served it mostly during the Christmas period. It is a light and refreshing change from the rich food we have indulged in over the holiday.

FRESH FIGS IN LITTLE BREAD BASKETS

To make 1:
1 fresh fig
1 rasher of back bacon
A little English mustard
1 bread roll (brown or white)
A little oil

Set oven to gas mark 6/200°C/400°F/Aga roasting oven.

Wrap the fig in the bacon rasher (like a jacket), and stand it in a lightly oiled shallow ovenproof dish.

Bake, uncovered, for 8-10 minutes or until the bacon is cooked.

Cut the top off the bread roll and scoop out the centre to form a cavity.

Place it on a greased baking tray and bake until brown and crisp (4-5 minutes).

Remove from oven and spread a little home-made mustard on the base before placing the baked fig inside.

Pour any pan juices over the fig.

LAZY COOK TIPS

This is a good combination of sweet and savoury flavours.

Secure the bacon ends with a wooden cocktail stick (avoid piercing the fig) or, if baking several, place them close together in the dish with the loose bacon ends touching. This will prevent the bacon unwrapping during cooking.

When the fig is sliced into, the juices escape and flavour and moisten the bread basket.

Serve as a starter or light meal with a watercress garnish. Keep the unused bread and make into breadcrumbs (see p223).

Smoked Salmon & Prawn Parcels with a Peppered Cream Sauce

Makes 4

4 slices smoked salmon
3 tablespoons of double cream
2 teaspoons of wholegrain mustard
A few pinches of ground white pepper
1 teaspoon of horseradish cream
100 g (4 oz) cooked prawns
1 hard-boiled egg (chopped)
Freshly chopped parsley
Chives
1 packet of peppered Boursin cheese
1-2 tablespoons of milk

Add the mustard, pepper and horseradish to the cream and whip to a soft peak.

Stir in the prawns, chopped egg and parsley, and pile into the centre of each smoked salmon slice. Gather the slice of salmon together (like a pouch) and secure by tying with a strand of chive.

Warm the Boursin and milk together in a pan and stir over a gentle heat until the Boursin has melted and the consistency is runny.

To serve, place the salmon pouches along the centre of a serving dish (or on individual plates) and pour the Boursin sauce around.

Lazy Cook Tips

Serve this recipe as a starter with fresh bread and butter, or serve as a light lunch with salad and fresh bread or rolls.

Melted Boursin makes an excellent instant sauce - very 'Lazy Cook'.

Lazy Cook Notes

FISH

My childhood was spent living next door to a fish and chip shop. I would often wake to the sound of the potatoes being peeled by the owner before he went off to do a day's work in a factory.

In those days the choice of fish and chips was, of course, battered cod, plaice, and cods roe. And for a penny we kids could buy a bag of 'batters' – all the bits of batter that collected in the pan of fat – what a treat! I hope you will find my choice of fish recipes equally appealing even without the 'batters'!

FISH RECIPES

Baked Cod with Grapes Poached in Vanilla & Honey

Baked Fish Cake

Salmon Bake

Fish Pudding

Fish in Pastry

Fish Roll Served with a Tartare Sauce

Baked Mackerel Fillets with a Leek & Tomato Sauce
on a Bed of Nutty Brown Rice

Baked Cod with Almonds & a Fresh Plum Sauce

Baked Trout with an Anchovy & Tomato Sauce

Fish Chowder

Fish Fillets with Spinach & Parma Ham

Mackerel Fillets with Baked Pear

Summer Platter

Shellfish with Rice

Salmon Steaks with a Melon Cup Garnish

Skate Wings with a Rhubarb Sauce

Tuna Steaks with a Mustard & Caper Cream Sauce

Fish & Bacon Pie served with Tapenade Sauce

Herring Fillets Baked in Orange Juice

Sweet Pickled Herrings

GUIDELINES FOR COOKING WITH FISH

WHEN IS IT COOKED?

It is difficult to give an exact time for cooking fish because it depends on the amount being cooked at one time.

My motto is: Undercooked fish is unpalatable, overcooked fish is a disaster!

Experience tells me that fish can be considered cooked when it is firm to the touch but there is a little movement. Each flake should be moist. It will continue to cook as it cools. I usually cook fish at a high temperature.

NUTRITIONAL CONTENT

Fish is more nutritious and has a better flavour if it is cooked with the skin on. Fish with high oil content is very good for you (e.g. mackerel, sardines, pilchards).

Tinned whole fish has a high nutritional content and should be included in a weekly diet.

BAKED COD WITH GRAPES POACHED IN VANILLA & HONEY

Serves 4
700 g (1½ lb) fillet of cod
25 g (1 oz) of butter
50 g (2 oz) of fresh or dried breadcrumbs (see p223)
For the grapes see recipe below

Set the oven to gas mark 6/200°C/400°F/Aga roasting oven.

Cover the base of a shallow ovenproof dish with a film of cold water. Wipe the fish with damp kitchen roll before placing it, skin-side down, into the dish. Sprinkle with breadcrumbs and dot with shavings of butter before baking in the preheated oven for 10-15 minutes, or until the fish is firm to the touch. Serve straight from the oven on individual hot plates, or in a hot serving dish. Place the grapes and juices on top and around.

GRAPES POACHED IN VANILLA & HONEY

50 ml (2 fl oz) of water
1 teaspoon of runny honey
½ teaspoon of vanilla extract
225 g (8 oz) of green or red seedless grapes

Pour the water into a pan, add the honey and vanilla, and stir over a gentle heat until it is dissolved. Add the grapes, cover and simmer gently for 5 minutes. Serve hot or cold with a fish or meat recipe.

LAZY COOK TIPS

The fish can be baked in one piece or cut into portions. To save time, poach the grapes while the fish is baking.

BAKED FISH CAKE

No Oil Needed!

I like to serve this as a light lunch. Accompany it with fresh bread or rolls and a good mixed green salad. It's a colourful presentation of fish and full of lovely flavours.

Serves 6
2 rainbow trout fillets
6 tomatoes
Fresh basil leaves
4 mushrooms (sliced)
Freshly ground black pepper
6-8 anchovy fillets preserved in oil

Set the oven to gas mark 6/200°C/400°F/Aga roasting oven.

Line the sides and base of a 900 g (2 lb) loaf tin with a strip of foil slightly overlapping each end. Using one or more fillets, cover the base – skin-side down and patching where necessary. Top with thick slices of tomato and season with freshly ground black pepper, basil leaves and then mushroom slices. Continue layering the ingredients until the last fish fillet is added – skin-side up, and crisscross this with anchovies to make a lattice pattern.

Drizzle with a little of the anchovy oil before baking in the preheated oven for 15-20 minutes or until the fish is firm to the touch (see p77). Allow to cool for a few minutes then cover with a piece of foil and press down lightly to compact the cooked layers.

To remove from the tin, loosen the sides using a palette knife. Then, by holding the overlapping foil ends, slide or lift from the foil strip onto a serving plate and pour all the remaining juices around. Cut into slices to serve (hot or cold).

==

LAZY COOK TIPS

This recipe can also be made using mackerel fillets. Make sure all bones are removed before assembling. Place the filling ingredients evenly over the fish and not all in the centre. Use a serrated knife to slice – it cuts best when cold.

==

SALMON BAKE

An ideal recipe for a quick supper.

Serves 4-6
40 g (1½ oz) of butter
1 medium-sized onion (skinned and finely chopped)
25 g (1 oz) of plain flour
300 ml (10 fl oz) of whole milk
50 ml (2 fl oz) of vermouth or dry white wine
415 g tin of red salmon (John West or similar)
½ teaspoon of dried oregano (or 1 teaspoon of fresh marjoram if available)
150 ml (5 fl oz) of single cream
Freshly ground white pepper
3 large eggs (hard-boiled, shelled and quartered)
175 g (6 oz) of closed cup mushrooms (wiped and sliced)
1 tablespoon of capers (from a jar)
50 g (2 oz) of Stilton cheese (crumbled)

Set the oven to gas mark 6/200°C/400°F/Aga roasting oven.

Melt the butter in a large pan over a gentle heat.

Add the prepared onion, cover and cook for 1-2 minutes, or until the onion begins to soften.

Stir in the flour and continue cooking for approximately 2 minutes.

Add the milk, wine, herbs and the juices from the tin of salmon, and stir until smooth, then simmer until the sauce begins to thicken (1-2 minutes).

Stir in the cream and season with freshly ground white pepper.

Remove the pan from the heat.

Place the salmon (broken into pieces), the prepared eggs, mushrooms and capers (strained from the juices), into a large, shallow, ovenproof dish.

Cover with the sauce and crumble the cheese on top.

Bake in the preheated oven for 20-30 minutes or until hot and bubbling.

Serve straight from the oven with peas, rice, pasta or warm bread or rolls. This is a great, quick family recipe.

LAZY COOK TIPS

It is possible for this recipe to be prepared in advance (add the cheese before reheating).

When cold, cover and store in a fridge or cold larder.

Reheating from cold will take a little longer; even though it might be bubbling around the edge of the dish, test that the centre is also hot by spooning a little out.

Other varieties of tinned fish can be included in this recipe (e.g. mussels, cockles, shrimps etc.)

If any are preserved in vinegar, rinse them under a cold tap before adding to the recipe.

FISH PUDDING

Serves 4
300 ml (10 fl oz) of milk
1 medium-sized onion (skinned and finely chopped)
Several good pinches of ground cloves
Freshly ground white pepper
450 g (1 lb) of skinless white fish fillet (or smoked haddock)
2 large eggs
175 g (6 oz) of grated cheese mixed with freshly chopped parsley
6-8 medium slices of bread (buttered)

Warm 100 ml (4 fl oz) of the milk in a pan over a gentle heat. Add the ground cloves, pepper and prepared onion. Pop the fish on top, cover the pan and simmer for approximately 5 minutes, then break the fish into flakes.

Butter (or oil) a 1 litre (about 2 pint) soufflé or pie dish, and line the base with buttered bread slices. Remove a portion of the fish and onion mix from the pan with a slotted spoon and layer it on top of the bread. Top with grated cheese and then another layer of bread. Continue this layering process until all of the ingredients are used, ending with bread sprinkled with cheese as the final layer.

Add the remaining milk to the pan juices and warm. Whisk the eggs a little before whisking them into the warmed milk, and pour this, through a sieve, onto the layered ingredients.

Press down with a fork and, if possible, leave for 30 minutes to 1 hour before baking at gas mark 4/180°C/350°F/Aga baking oven for 30-40 minutes or until well risen and brown on top. Serve hot.

LAZY COOK TIPS

This can be made in any ovenproof dish if you do not have a soufflé or suitable pie dish. Stand the chosen dish on a baking tray to bake. Use up odd ends of cheese of mixed flavours grating soft cheeses before hard ones. This recipe can also be made using shellfish.

FISH IN PASTRY

I am always reluctant to quote preparation times for my recipes but I can say with confidence that this meal can be prepared for the oven in Mo-ments — read on!

Serves 6-8
425 g packet of frozen ready-rolled puff pastry
(2 sheets approximately 280 x 215 cm each)
750 g packet of frozen boneless white fish fillets

QUICK
FIX

Set oven to gas mark 7/220°C /425°F/Aga roasting oven.

Defrost the pastry. Wrap 2 fillets in each sheet of pastry (like sausage rolls). Dampen the edges with a little cold water to seal together and put onto 2 lightly oiled baking trays (Swiss roll type), sealed ends down.

Bake in the preheated oven for 30-35 minutes or until the pastry has puffed up and is a biscuit colour.

Cut each into 3 or 4 portions and serve straight from the oven, or place on a hot serving dish.

Serve with oven chips (cooked at the same time as the fish rolls), frozen peas and tomato ketchup.

LAZY COOK TIPS

I find that frozen fish shrinks as it cooks so pack as much as you can into the roll.

Keep a packet of frozen ready-rolled puff pastry, frozen fish fillets, oven chips and frozen peas in the freezer and the rest is child's play!

FISH ROLL SERVED WITH A TARTARE SAUCE

I created this recipe when monkfish was first made popular by TV chefs at which time it cost around £4 a kilo – it is now nearer £24 a kilo. Even so, I still think it is the best fish to use in this recipe for a special occasion, but you could be forgiven for using another not quite so expensive white fish too.

Serves 4 slices
225 g (8 oz) piece of salmon or trout fillet
225 g (8 oz) of monkfish fillet
4 strands of fennel fern (optional)
6 rashers of rindless bacon
A little olive oil

Set the oven to gas mark 6/200°C/400°F/Aga roasting oven.

Dry the fish on kitchen roll. Lightly oil the base of a shallow baking dish or tin.

Stretch each bacon rasher using a blunt knife and place on a board, slightly overlapping.

Top with the fennel fern, and then the fillets (placed side by side).

Enclose in the bacon rashers (like a double sausage roll) and place in the prepared dish, loose bacon ends down.

Lightly brush the bacon with oil and bake in the preheated oven for 20-25 minutes, or until the roll is firm to the touch in the centre.

Remove from the oven and, when cold, slice and serve with tartare sauce (see opposite).

Serve with new potatoes and salad as a main course, or cut into thin slices and garnish with a little watercress or lamb's lettuce to serve as a starter. Serve the sauce separately.

Tartare Sauce

4 tablespoons of mayonnaise (see p185)
1 tablespoon of capers (roughly chopped)
1 teaspoon of horseradish cream
Freshly ground white pepper

Mix all of the ingredients together in a bowl. Serve immediately, or store in an airtight container in the fridge. Use within 5 days.

Increase quantities to make a larger amount.

Lazy Cook Tips

Each fish fillet should be of a similar thickness and length.

If necessary, secure any loose bacon ends with a wooden cocktail stick.

The dish can be served hot, but it slices better when cold.

When cold, wrap in cling film and store in a fridge or cold larder. Use within 3 days.

Bring back to room temperature before serving.

Baked Mackerel Fillets with a Leek & Tomato Sauce on a Bed of Nutty Brown Rice

A very colourful dish — everything about this recipe is healthy eating.

Serves 4

4 fresh mackerel fillets

1 leek

100 g (4 oz) of mushrooms (wiped and sliced)

1 x 400 g tin of chopped tomatoes

1 teaspoon of tomato purée

50 ml (2 fl oz) of stock or water

A dash of wine (red or white)

A pinch of sugar

Several good pinches of mixed dried herbs

Freshly ground white pepper

A handful of pitted black olives

Freshly chopped parsley

Boiled brown rice (see p25)

Set the oven to gas mark 6/200°C/400°F/Aga roasting oven.

Pour a film of cold water into a shallow ovenproof dish and add the fillets, skin-side down. Bake in the preheated oven for 4-5 minutes, or until firm to the touch. Remove from the oven and keep warm.

Top and tail and thinly slice the leek. Wash under a cold running tap, then cook for a minute in a little boiling water, in a covered pan. Add all of the remaining ingredients (except the parsley and rice) and simmer for a few minutes.

To serve, spread the cooked rice over the base of a large, hot serving dish and place the baked mackerel on top. Bring the sauce back to a simmer, spoon a little over the mackerel and scatter with parsley. Dish up the remainder separately.

Lazy Cook Tips

A good fishmonger or supermarket will fillet the fresh fish for you.

Baked Cod with Almonds & a Fresh Plum Sauce

Serves 4
700 g (1½ lb) of fillet of cod
25 g (1 oz) of butter
50 g (2 oz) of flaked almonds (lightly browned)
Fresh plum sauce (see below)

Set oven to gas mark 6/200°C/400°F/Aga roasting oven.

Cover the base of a shallow ovenproof dish with a film of cold water and add the fish (skin-side down). Top with shavings of butter, then with a scattering of flaked almonds. Bake in a preheated oven for 10-15 minutes or until the fish is firm to the touch.

Serve straight from the baking dish or arrange the fish in the centre of a hot serving dish and pour some of the plum sauce around. Serve the remainder separately.

Fresh Plum Sauce

900 g (2 lb) of plums (washed, stoned and sliced)
50 ml (2 oz) of sweet Martini
Runny honey to taste
A few drops of almond essence

Simmer the plum slices in a covered pan with the Martini until they begin to soften. Taste and stir in a little runny honey if the flavour is too sharp, then stir in 2-3 drops of almond essence. Serve hot or cold.

Lazy Cook Tips

The fish can be baked in one piece or cut into portions – a whole fillet will take longer to bake than smaller pieces. Make the sauce while the fish is baking. Always keep a supply of lightly browned flaked almonds in stock – brown in the oven or under a grill and store in a jar or airtight container.

BAKED TROUT WITH AN ANCHOVY & TOMATO SAUCE

QUICK
FIX

Serves 4
700 g (1½ lb) fillet of trout with skin
Freshly ground black pepper
A little white wine (optional)

Set the oven to gas mark 6/200°C/400°F/Aga roasting oven.

Cover the base of a shallow ovenproof dish with a film of cold water or wine.

Dry the fish on kitchen roll then cut the fillet into 4 equally sized pieces and place in the dish, skin-side down. Season with freshly ground black pepper and bake in the preheated oven for 5-8 minutes, or until the fillets are firm to the touch. Make the sauce (see below) while the fish is cooking.

To serve, arrange the fillets on individual hot plates or one large serving dish. Serve the sauce separately.

ANCHOVY & TOMATO SAUCE

The Quickest Ever!

2 tablespoons of tomato ketchup
1 teaspoon of sun-dried tomato paste
4-6 fresh anchovy fillets (crush in a pestle and mortar).
1-2 teaspoons of runny honey
Vegetable stock or water

Place all the ingredients in a pan and stir over a gentle heat until simmering. Thin down with stock or water to the desired consistency. Serve hot or cold.

This sauce complements any hot or cold savoury food.

LAZY COOK TIPS

If the fillet is in one whole piece it may take longer to cook, but do make sure to avoid overcooking. For the sauce I prefer to use anchovy fillets preserved in oil and sold by weight.

FISH CHOWDER

A welcoming recipe to serve on a cold winter's day.

Serves 6
1 large onion (skinned and chopped)
100 g (4 oz) of unsmoked bacon (cut into pieces)
2 sticks of celery (sliced)
100 g (4 oz) of mushrooms (wiped and sliced)
900 g (2 lb) of potatoes (peeled and cut into bite-sized pieces)
1 x 400 g tin of sweetcorn (juices drained)
700 g (1 ½ lb) of cod
2 tablespoons of flour seasoned with freshly ground white pepper
150 ml (5 fl oz) of single cream
2 teaspoons of Dijon mustard
Generous handful of freshly chopped parsley

Soften the onion, bacon, celery and mushrooms in a small amount of boiling water in a large covered pan or casserole dish.

Add the potatoes and top up with sufficient cold water to cover.

Put the lid on the pan and allow to simmer until the potatoes are almost cooked, then add the sweetcorn.

Dry the fish on kitchen roll, then cut into bite-sized pieces and coat in the seasoned flour. Place them on top of the pan ingredients.

Bring back to a simmer, cover and continue simmering for 10 minutes or until the fish has cooked.

Stir in the cream, mustard and parsley and bring back to a simmer, before serving with warm rolls or chunks of bread.

LAZY COOK TIPS

Cod cheeks, which are often available from a good fishmonger, are excellent for this recipe.

If you cook by Aga the simmering process should be done in the simmering oven. Ideal for either lunch or supper.

FISH FILLETS WITH SPINACH & PARMA HAM

Serves 4
4 white fish fillets
1 tablespoon of white wine (optional)
Freshly ground black pepper
450 g (1 lb) of spinach (cooked)
8 wafer-thin slices of Parma or Black Forest ham

Set the oven to gas mark 6/200°C/400°F/Aga roasting oven.

Cover the base of a shallow ovenproof dish with a film of wine or water and add the fillets (skin-side down). Season with freshly ground pepper.

Bake in the preheated oven for 6-8 minutes, or until the fillets are firm to the touch.

Serve the fillets on individual hot plates, or arrange on one large, hot serving plate. Spoon any juices from the dish over each fillet before topping with the cooked spinach and crumpled ham slices.

You can serve this dish with pasta or rice tossed in a little oil and plenty of fresh herbs. Alternatively, serve it alongside a green salad.

LAZY COOK TIPS

This recipe looks stunning and the flavours are delicious.

The spinach can be cooked at the same time as the fish.

If serving with pasta or rice, allow extra time for these to be cooked.

Parma or Black Forest hams add an instant bacon flavour without even needing to be cooked! They will store for several days in a fridge and will add instant eye-catching presentation to most savoury dishes and salads – another Lazy Cook ingredient to add to your shopping list.

MACKEREL FILLETS
WITH BAKED PEAR

Serves 4
4 mackerel fillets
4 teaspoons of wholegrain mustard
2 large pears (peeled, cored and cut into quarters)
4 tablespoons of Calvados or ginger wine

Pour the Calvados (or ginger wine) into a pan and bring to the boil.

Add the prepared pears, cover and simmer for 5-10 minutes, or until the pears have softened.

Pour a film of cold water into a shallow ovenproof dish and add the fillets, skin-side down.

Spread the flesh with wholegrain mustard and bake in the preheated oven, uncovered, for 5-10 minutes or until firm to the touch.

Serve on individual hot plates or one large serving dish, with the pears and juice on top and around.

Serve with rice and a green vegetable of your choice.

Delicious in summer, served cold with salad and new potatoes.

LAZY COOK TIPS

The flavour of the pears offsets this oily fish perfectly.

Mackerel has a high nutritional value and should be included in your weekly diet.

SUMMER PLATTER

A perfect meal for summer or for an adult picnic.

Serves 8
1 packet of smoked salmon (minimum 8 slices)
1 bunch of rocket
Freshly ground black pepper
4 large eggs (hard-boiled)
8 fresh anchovy fillets
8 thin slices of Parma ham
8 rollmop herrings
8 strawberries (cut in halves)

Prepare the salmon rolls and eggs as follows:

Place a few rocket leaves on each salmon slice, season with freshly ground black pepper and roll up loosely.

Shell the hard-boiled eggs, cut them in half, and then curl a fresh anchovy fillet on top of each.

Arrange these, along with the remaining ingredients, in rows on a large platter and garnish with strawberry halves. Serve with salad, new potatoes, mayonnaise and vinaigrette (see p185).

LAZY COOK TIPS

Rollmop herrings can be bought ready-made in most supermarkets and delicatessens, and they are a very useful ingredient to keep in store – please make sure to refer to the 'use-by' date. I think the ham slices look far more decorative wrinkled up rather than leaving them flat. This is an excellent 'last-minute' summer meal which can, if more convenient, be prepared several hours in advance and stored in a fridge, covered with foil or cling film. Alternatively, if you are taking the platter with you on a picnic, the ingredients can be packed into plastic containers and presented as suggested in the recipe, or served directly onto plates at the venue. Large foil serving platters can be purchased from most supermarkets.

SHELLFISH WITH RICE

This is a Lazy Cook's paella. Cockles and mussels are amongst my favourite shellfish. My Gran, who lived with us, cooked mussels for my father and myself and taught us the importance of removing the beard, and discarding any opened shells before cooking. Since childhood I cannot visit a seaside promenade without buying a bag of cockles. Rice is also one of my favourite ingredients and I think that together they make a perfect combination of colours, textures and flavours.

Serves 4
225 g (8 oz) cooked rice (see p25)
¼ of a stick of celery (sliced thinly across the stalks)
4-6 spring onions (sliced thinly, including green stalks)
225 g (8 oz) mix of cooked shelled prawns, mussels, cockles
or other shellfish of your choice
Freshly chopped herbs
Freshly ground white pepper
Several pinches of curry powder
50 g (2 oz) of pistachio nuts (shelled)
4 tablespoons of mayonnaise or single cream

Mix all the ingredients together and serve as a starter in individual stemmed glasses, or in earthenware bowls as a light meal.

To serve hot, stir the ingredients into the cooked rice over a gentle heat adding single cream in place of mayonnaise.

LAZY COOK TIPS

If available throw in a handful of cooked mussels in their shells and serve directly from the pan for a rustic meal.

SALMON STEAKS WITH A MELON CUP GARNISH

I created this recipe for my sister Elsie who only eats fish, preferably without any sauce or garnish, and this was my way of adding a little interest to her meal.

Serves 4

4 middle fillet salmon steaks
Freshly ground black pepper
4 strands of fennel fern (optional)
1-2 tablespoons of white wine (optional)
4 melon cups (see opposite)

Set the oven to gas mark 6/200°C/400°F/Aga roasting oven.

Pour a film of water (or white wine) over the base of a shallow ovenproof dish.

Add the steaks (skin-side down), season each with freshly ground black pepper and top with a strand of fennel fern.

Bake in the preheated oven for 8-10 minutes, or until the steaks are firm to the touch at the thickest part.

Remove from the oven, strain off and reserve all the juices.

While the steaks are cooling, prepare the melon cups as directed.

To serve, put the steaks onto individual plates or one large serving dish and place the melon cups alongside or at the ends.

LAZY COOK TIPS

This is a good combination of flavours and a simple but eye-catching presentation, perfect for a summer lunch party.

The steaks can be cooked one or two days in advance and stored, covered, in a fridge or cold larder. Bring them back to room temperature before serving.

Melon Cups

Makes 4
2 small melons
12 cooked prawns in shells
A small bunch of red seedless grapes
A bunch of radishes (leave whole if small or cut into strips)
4 fresh mint leaves (cut into thin strips)
8 small strawberries

Cut each melon in half and remove and discard all seeds.

Using a teaspoon, scoop out the flesh into a sieve placed over a basin in order to collect the juices.

Cut a thin sliver from the base of each cup to enable them to stand firm and 'hang' 3 prawns from each.

To the reserved melon juice, add approximately half the flesh, the reserved fish juices, a handful of grapes, several small radishes, the cut mint leaves and the strawberries.

Stir them together before packing into the cups. Serve with cold cooked fish.

Lazy Cook Tips

All remaining fruit and juices can form the base of a fresh fruit salad.

Frozen prawns in shells can be purchased from a fishmonger or supermarket – I recommend several of these are kept in your freezer; they will give an instant, eye-catching garnish to many fish recipes.

SKATE WINGS WITH
A RHUBARB SAUCE

Serves 4
4 skate wings
25 g (1 oz) of butter (preferably unsalted)
A bunch of watercress
Rhubarb sauce

Heat a large non-stick frying or sauté pan, then add the butter. Once this has melted add the steaks and cook for 2-3 minutes on each side. Serve straight from the pan on individual plates or on one large platter with a garnish of watercress. Serve the sauce separately.

LAZY COOK TIPS

For a very long time I didn't buy this fish, thinking it was mostly bones, but what appear to be large bones are the markings of the flesh. It has a sweet, delicate flavour and this is just one of the many ways I serve it, taking advantage of the early rhubarb season.

RHUBARB SAUCE

Several sticks of young rhubarb
Clear honey
Orange flower water

Wash and top and tail the rhubarb before cutting into slices approximately 5mm (¼ inch) in thickness. Soften in a little boiling water in a covered pan. Sweeten with honey and flavour with a few dashes of orange flower water. Serve hot or cold.

LAZY COOK TIPS

Avoid adding too much honey, especially when serving with savoury recipes.

TUNA STEAKS WITH A MUSTARD & CAPER CREAM SAUCE

Serves 4
4 tuna steaks
A little olive oil
Freshly ground pepper
Mustard & caper cream sauce

QUICK FIX

Heat a large non-stick frying or sauté pan. Brush each steak on one side with oil and season with a little freshly ground pepper and cook in the hot pan for 2 minutes. Oil and season the uncooked side before turning and also cooking for 2 minutes. Remove from the pan and keep warm. Scrape up the pan juices, add the mustard cream sauce ingredients and the capers and whisk until boiling. Serve the steaks with a little sauce poured over each.

MUSTARD & CAPER CREAM SAUCE

An excellent example of using convenient store cupboard ingredients. Vary the flavour by replacing the capers with cocktail onions, chopped anchovies or herbs.

1 teaspoon of Dijon mustard
1 teaspoon of wholegrain mustard
1 teaspoon of sun-dried tomato purée
2 teaspoons of capers
1 tablespoon of double cream
150 ml (5 fl oz) of stock (vegetable, chicken or fish)

Combine all the ingredients together in a pan and whisk until boiling. Serve hot or cold.

LAZY COOK TIPS

It is important not to overcook tuna as it becomes very dry and loses its delicate flavour.

FISH & BACON PIE
SERVED WITH TAPENADE SAUCE

Serves 4
450 g (1 lb) of white fish fillets
50 ml (2 fl oz) of white wine (or water)
Parsley and thyme forcemeat (see opposite)
8 rashers of rindless streaky bacon (cut into 3 cm/1 inch lengths)
A little lemon juice

Set the oven to gas mark 6/200°C/400°F/Aga roasting oven.

Pour the wine (or water) into a large shallow ovenproof dish, add the fish and sprinkle with lemon juice. Add the forcemeat and then top with the bacon pieces. Place in the preheated oven and bake for 10-15 minutes, or until the fish is cooked (see p77).

LAZY COOK TIPS

The fish can be broken into flakes or left in whole pieces before cooking. Be sure to remove any visible bones.

TAPENADE SAUCE

60 ml (2 fl oz) of white wine
60 ml (2 fl oz) of fish or vegetable stock
2 teaspoons of tapenade paste
1 spray of fresh fennel fern (if available)
2 teaspoons of double cream

Pour the wine and stock into a pan and boil to reduce by half. Stir in the remaining ingredients and serve.

LAZY COOK TIPS

Tear the fennel from the main stalk to make into small strands. Keep the sauce covered in a fridge or cold larder and use within 3 days. Tapenade paste is available from supermarkets or delicatessens.

Parsley & Thyme Forcemeat

175 g (6 oz) of bread
½ teaspoon each of dried parsley and dried thyme
Freshly ground white pepper
1 large egg
1 lemon (zest and juice)

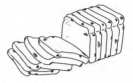

Set the oven to gas mark 4/180°C/350°F/Aga baking oven.

In a food processor, blend the pieces of bread until they form breadcrumbs.

Add the parsley and thyme and process for a few seconds.

Add the egg, the grated zest from the lemon and a little of the juice and process it further until it blends together.

Spread the resulting paste into a lightly oiled ovenproof dish and bake in the preheated oven for 10-15 minutes.

Lazy Cook Tips

The texture should be a sticky breadcrumb consistency before it is cooked. Add more lemon juice if necessary.

Allow the forcemeat to rest for 30 minutes before baking if time allows.

Use a good handful of fresh parsley and thyme if available.

To serve with roast chicken shape into little balls and place on a lightly oiled ovenproof dish or tin tray for baking.

HERRING FILLETS BAKED IN ORANGE JUICE

Serves 8
4 herring fillets (washed and dried on kitchen roll)
8-12 anchovies preserved in oil
A small bunch of fresh coriander
50ml (2 fl oz) white wine
50ml (2 fl oz) fresh orange juice
1 teaspoon tomato purée

Set oven to gas mark 6/200°C/400°F/Aga roasting oven.

Cut and discard the small fin from the middle of each herring. Place in a shallow ovenproof dish, skin-side down, and top each fillet with 2 or 3 anchovies.

Pour the wine and orange juice into a small pan. Whisk in the tomato purée and bring to the boil.

Pour the liquid over the herring fillets and scatter with fresh coriander.

Bake, uncovered, for 7-10 minutes or until the fillets are firm to the touch.

Serve hot or cold, with seasonal vegetables or salad.

LAZY COOK TIPS

Herring fillets are cheap and nutritious. I recommend using anchovy fillets preserved in oil and bought by weight from most supermarkets or delicatessen counters.

SWEET PICKLED HERRINGS

The perfect summer lunch: Sweet Pickled Herrings with a mixed salad and fresh bread, a glass of rosé, and for pudding, Raspberry Sponge (see p202). Three days in the making – but well worth the wait!

Serves 8

4 herring fillets (washed and dried on kitchen roll)

1 large onion

MARINADE INGREDIENTS:

75 ml (3 fl oz) of water

75 ml (3 fl oz) of wine vinegar

SAUCE INGREDIENTS:

50 ml (2 fl oz) of olive oil

50 ml (2 fl oz) of wine vinegar

1 tablespoon of tomato purée

1 tablespoon of sun-dried tomato paste

2 tablespoons of warm water

1 tablespoon of demerara sugar

1 level tablespoon of runny honey

½ teaspoon of crushed white peppercorns

2 dried bay leaves

½ teaspoon of dried dill

Cut and discard the small fin from the middle of each herring, then slice each in half. Place in a dish, skin-side down, and pour over the marinade ingredients. Cover with foil and store in a fridge or cold larder for 48 hours.

After this time, drain and discard the marinade. Skin the onion and slice very finely and spread over the herrings. Mix all the sauce ingredients together and pour over the fish. Cover the dish with foil and store in a fridge or cold larder for 24 hours before serving. Use within 3 days.

LAZY COOK TIPS

It is very important to make this recipe using 'day fresh' herrings – purchase these from a reputable fishmonger or supermarket.

Lazy Cook Notes

MEAT

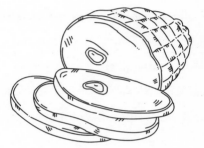

I was recently taken aback when much of the meat I have always cooked suddenly displayed a label 'forgotten cuts'. 'Where have these people been all these years?' was my reaction. Shoulder of lamb, ox tongue, belly pork (and why does it never have buttons these days?), are amongst the most tasty and nutritious meats available because of their bone and fat content.

In this section you will find many recipes using cheaper cuts, do try them, I think you will find their flavour far outweighs that of the most expensive meats on display — I should know, I was brought up on them.

MEAT RECIPES

Beef Slices in a Tomato & Mustard Sauce

Braised Beef with Apricots & Black Olives

Sirloin Steaks with a Peppered Cream Sauce

Beef Casserole

Braised Silverside Slices with Pickled Walnuts

Beef & Bangers Casserole

Daube (Beef Casserole)

Fillet Steak with an Artichoke & Apricot Compote

Steak, Kidney & Mushroom Pie

Stew and Dumplings

Ox Cheek

Minced Beef

Minced Meat Stick

Osso Buco (Veal Shin Bones)

Veal & Bacon Parcels with a Sun-dried Tomato Sauce

Pork Fillet with Sun-dried Tomatoes & Black Olives

Pork Cooked in a Piquant Sauce

Pork Steaks with an Orange & Ginger Sauce

Pork Steaks with Autumn Fruits

Pork Belly Slices with a Mustard Pickle Sauce

Meat Recipes Continued

Gammon Steaks Cooked in a Tomato Sauce

Ham & Leek Pie

Ham & Beef Hash

Ham with a Black Cherry Sauce

Bangers & Mash with a Pickle Topping

Lamb Fillets with a Garlic Cream Sauce

Crown of Lamb Served with a Red Wine & Pesto Sauce

Devilled Lamb

Lamb's Liver

Red Wine Gravy

Spicy Lamb Casserole

Venison Sausages Wrapped in Aubergine & Bacon
with a Cranberry Sauce

Braised Venison

Savoury Meat Batter

Village Pie

Simmering of Meats

Chicken & Bacon Rolls with Sun-dried Tomatoes

Chicken Breasts Cooked in Red Wine and Thyme

Chicken with Apricots & Almonds

Guidelines for Cooking Meat

Coat in seasoned flour

This is done before ingredients are browned or sealed in hot oil – I mostly use olive oil but the choice is yours. It is important to dry the ingredients first on kitchen roll (wet ingredients will not seal). Coat the ingredients all over in the seasoned flour and then shake off all excess – I do this by tossing the ingredients from hand to hand. Once they are coated, immediately place them into the hot oil. Ingredients are browned in hot oil to 'seal in' the flavour.

Excess fat

Remove excess fat from hot cooked ingredients by tilting the pan and spooning out the fat/oil. When cooked ingredients are cold all excess fat will rise to the surface. Remove with a knife before reheating.

Heating oil or dripping

A few grains of flour dropped into the pan should sizzle when the oil or dripping is hot enough to take the ingredients to be browned/sealed.

Pots & Pans

In addition to a good set of saucepans of varying sizes, I especially recommend pans that can be used on top of the cooker then put into the oven. These are mostly cast iron and I find them invaluable – always buy from a reputable kitchen shop. Amongst my other favourite pans are:

- A large sauté pan with a lid – these are roughly 23 cm/9½ inches in diameter and 7 cm/3 inches in depth.

- A large non-stick frying pan with a removable handle. This, and many other pans in this range, are lightweight but still do the job of cast iron. A high-quality kitchen shop should be able to advise on this range which I recommend.

- Casserole dishes with fitted lids – small through to large.

- Shallow ovenproof dishes of varying sizes that can be taken from oven to table are essential.

Never add cold liquids to a hot pan.

Reheating from cold

I am a great believer in the saying 'yesterday's stew is best'. The flavour of many recipes is improved by allowing them to rest for 24 hours or longer before serving: it gives the ingredients time to blend, resulting in an improved flavour.

Once cooked and allowed to cool, cover the dish with a lid or foil, and place in a fridge or cold larder until ready to reheat.

To reheat, cover, and place in a hot oven (gas mark 6/200°C/400°F/ Aga roasting oven) for 10 minutes or until it is hot throughout. Test by spooning out a little from the centre – this is important because often the outer liquid is bubbling but the centre remains lukewarm.

When hot throughout, reduce the temperature to gas mark 3/ 160°C/325°F/Aga simmering oven (or as the recipe advises) and continue cooking until it is needed for serving. The time will depend on the quantity of ingredients to be reheated.

If a single portion is to be reheated, this can be done on a hob following the above directions.

Seasonings

Use pepper or spices and herbs in place of salt.

Soften in water

I often recommend softening onions and other vegetables in a little hot water. This will produce a few concentrated teaspoons of stock which will add goodness and flavour to your recipe without a trace of fat.

Soften the vegetables in a covered pan with only a little bit of water. It takes 1-2 minutes, depending on the amount of vegetables being softened.

Wine

Boil wine to reduce and to burn off the alcohol, leaving the flavour of the wine. This is often shown by putting a flame to the hot wine but I do not recommend this method in a domestic kitchen.

WHEN IS IT COOKED?

POULTRY

Undercooked, pink chicken and turkey should not be served but overcooked poultry is dry and loses much of the flavour.

Test by piercing the thickest part with a skewer; it is cooked when the juices run clear.

MEAT & GAME

Like chicken, to determine if pork is cooked, test by piercing the thickest part with a skewer. If the juices run clear it is done.

Other meats can be cooked to your personal liking: rare, medium or well done. Follow the directions in the recipe and adjust the cooking time accordingly.

Game is often casseroled or slow cooked. Follow the directions in the recipe or the suppliers' instructions.

OFFAL

Calves' or lambs' liver and kidneys require little cooking – when the blood seeps out they are done.

Ox kidney is usually cooked for longer, in a casserole or slow cooker.

BEEF SLICES IN A
TOMATO & MUSTARD SAUCE
A recipe using cheaper cuts.

Serves 4

4 slices of braising steak (not less than 1 cm/½ inch thick)

1 tablespoon of olive oil or dripping

1 tablespoon of flour, seasoned with freshly ground black pepper

4 large shallots (or medium-sized onions)

300 ml can of tomato juice

4 teaspoons of wholegrain mustard

1 bay leaf

A good pinch of mixed dried herbs

Set the oven to gas mark 3/160°C/325°F/Aga simmering oven.

Heat the oil or dripping in a sauté or large pan. Remove any excess fat before drying the meat on kitchen roll and coating lightly in the seasoned flour. Add to the pan and brown for 1-2 minutes on each side in the hot fat.

While the meat is browning, skin the onions, leaving them whole. Remove the meat from the pan and mop up any excess fat with kitchen roll. Add the tomato juice and mustard and stir, scraping up any residue which may have stuck to the base.

Return the meat, onions, bay leaf and herbs to the pan. Bring to a simmer, cover and transfer to the preheated oven for 1½-2 hours, or until the meat is tender. Serve from the pan with vegetables of your choice.

LAZY COOK TIPS

This is a good recipe for using cheaper cuts, most of which have an excellent flavour. The fat removed before cooking can be rendered down in a low oven to make dripping (once cooled, store in a fridge). I recommend this recipe is made in advance and allowed to rest in a fridge or cold larder for a day or two before reheating to serve. This is an ideal recipe if you are cooking for one, as it can easily be reheated in portions as and when required.

BRAISED BEEF WITH APRICOTS & BLACK OLIVES

A recipe using cheaper cuts.

Serves 4

4 slices of braising steak (not less than 1 cm/½ inch thick)
1 tablespoon of olive oil or dripping
1 tablespoon of flour, seasoned with freshly ground black pepper
½ bottle of red wine
100 ml (4 fl oz) of stock
1 teaspoon of sun-dried tomato paste
2 bay leaves
Several sprays of fresh thyme (or ½ teaspoon of dried)
1 teaspoon of runny honey
12-16 whole dried apricots
16-20 pitted olives

Set the oven to gas mark 3/160°C/325°F/Aga simmering oven.

Heat the oil or dripping in a sauté or large pan. Remove any excess fat from the meat before drying it on kitchen roll and coating lightly in the seasoned flour.

Add to the pan and brown for 1-2 minutes on each side in the hot fat.

Remove the meat from the pan and mop up any excess fat with kitchen roll.

Add the wine and stock to the pan and scrape up any residue from the base before bringing it to the boil. Stir in the tomato paste, bay leaves, thyme and honey.

Return the meat slices to the pan and bring to a simmer.

Cover and put into the preheated oven for 1½-2 hours (or until the meat is tender).

Towards the end of cooking add the apricots and olives and allow it to cook for a further 30 minutes.

To serve, arrange the meat slices directly onto hot serving plates, or down the centre of one large serving dish.

Remove the apricots and olives with a slotted spoon and place on top.

Boil the remaining sauce until it reduces and begins to thicken. Spoon a little over the meat and serve the remainder separately.

LAZY COOK TIPS

I like to serve this with a dish of roasted winter vegetables — potatoes, pumpkin, parsnips and small whole onions (see p159). This is another good recipe for those flavoursome cheaper cuts.

The fat removed before cooking can be rendered down in a low oven to make dripping (once cooled, store in a fridge).

I recommend this recipe is made in advance and allowed to rest in a fridge or cold larder for a day or two before reheating to serve.

This is an ideal recipe if you are cooking for one, as it can easily be reheated in portions as and when required. Serve within 3 days of making.

Sirloin Steaks with a Peppered Cream Sauce

QUICK
FIX

Serves 4
4 sirloin steaks (not less than 1 cm/½ inch thick)
Olive oil
Freshly ground black pepper
Peppered cream sauce (see below)

Heat a sauté or large frying pan, dry the steaks on kitchen roll and brush one side with oil and season with pepper before adding to the hot pan

Time the cooking according to whether you like rare, medium or well done.

Before turning the steaks, oil and season the upper side.

Remove from the pan and put onto individual hot plates or one large serving dish, spooning any remaining juices over each steak.

Serve the sauce separately.

Peppered Cream Sauce

1 large packet of Boursin peppered cream cheese
1 tablespoon of milk

Warm the cheese and milk in a pan over a gentle heat and whisk until smooth. Serve hot or cold.

Lazy Cook Tips

Recommended cooking times:

Rare – 2 minutes on each side.

Medium rare – 3 minutes on each side.

Well done – 5 minutes on each side.

BEEF CASSEROLE

Serves 4

1 large onion (skinned and chopped)
450 g (1 lb) of diced braising steak
175 g (6 oz) of chorizo slices (skinned)
150 ml (5 fl oz) of red wine (optional)
150 ml (5 fl oz) of meat stock
227 g tin of chopped tomatoes in natural juices
½ teaspoon of mixed dried herbs
Freshly ground black pepper

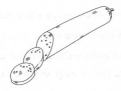

Set oven at gas mark 6/200°C/400°F/Aga roasting oven.

Heat a little water in a medium-sized casserole dish or pan with a lid.

Add the onion, cover and cook for a few minutes until it begins to soften.

Add all the remaining ingredients, stir, then cover, and put into the preheated oven for 15-20 minutes or until it begins to simmer.

Reduce the oven temperature to gas mark 3/160°C/325°F/Aga simmering oven and continue to cook for 1 hour or until the meat is tender.

LAZY COOK TIPS

Like so many of my recipes, once cooked this can be left to cool and then stored in a fridge or cold larder for a few days before serving. Use within 4 days.

Before reheating, remove any fat which will have risen to the surface.

BRAISED SILVERSIDE SLICES WITH PICKLED WALNUTS

Serves 4

4 slices of silverside of beef (not less than 1 cm/½ inch thick)
1 tablespoon of flour seasoned with freshly ground black pepper
1 tablespoon of olive oil or 25 g (1 oz) of dripping
1 medium-sized onion (skinned and thinly sliced)
150 ml (5 fl oz) of red wine
150 ml (5 fl oz) of stock
½ teaspoon of dried herbes de Provence
1 teaspoon of wholegrain mustard
8-12 pickled walnuts

Set oven to gas mark 3/160°C/325°F/Aga simmering oven.

Heat the oil or dripping in a sauté or large pan.

Dry the beef on kitchen roll, trim off any excess fat, and then lightly coat each in the seasoned flour.

Add to the pan and brown for 1-2 minutes on each side in the hot fat, and then remove.

Add a little hot water to the pan and scrape up any residue from the base before adding the prepared onion.

Cover and cook until it begins to soften.

Remove the onion from the pan, add the wine and stock, and boil to reduce by half.

Stir in the herbs and mustard, return the meat and onion and bring to a simmer.

Cover and put into the preheated oven for 1½-2 hours or until the meat is tender.

Towards the end of cooking, add the pickled walnuts and cook for a further 10 minutes.

To serve, put the meat slices onto individual hot serving plates or down the centre of one large serving dish.

Remove the onion and walnuts with a slotted spoon and place them on top and around the meat.

Boil the remaining sauce until it reduces and thickens, spoon a little over the meat and serve the remainder separately.

LAZY COOK TIPS

This is another example of making cheaper cuts interesting.

It's an ideal recipe if cooking for one because it can be reheated in individual portions.

The fat removed before cooking should be rendered down in a low-heated oven to make dripping (once cooled, store in a fridge).

This recipe can be made in advance and when cold stored, covered, in a fridge or cold larder for a day or two before reheating.

Serve within 3 days. To reheat refer to guidelines on p108.

BEEF & BANGERS CASSEROLE

Prepare a day in advance of serving.

Serves 6

1 tablespoon of olive oil

6 x 1 cm (½ inch) thick slices of 'feather' steak

1 tablespoon of plain flour seasoned with freshly ground black pepper

6 beef (or gamey) sausages

½ bottle of red wine

300 ml (10 fl oz) of stock

1 teaspoon of herbes de Provence (or mixed dried herbs)

4 oz of dried sun-dried tomatoes

Set the oven to gas mark 3/160°C/325°F/ Aga simmering oven.

Heat the oil in a large casserole dish. Dry the steaks on kitchen roll, trim off any excess fat, and then lightly coat each in the seasoned flour.

Add to the hot fat and brown for 1-2 minutes on each side and then remove from the pan.

Scrape the residue from the base of the pan, add the sausages and brown them a little before removing.

Cover the base of the pan with hot water and again scrape up any residue before adding the wine and stock.

Boil for a minute or two to reduce, and then return the steaks, sausages, tomatoes and herbs to the pan.

Bring to a simmer, cover and put into the preheated oven for 1½-2 hours, or until the meat is tender.

Remove from the oven and allow it to cool. Cover and store in a fridge or cold larder.

TO REHEAT BEFORE SERVING:

Set the oven to gas mark 6/200°C/400°F/ Aga roasting oven.

Remove all fat from the surface, cover the pan and put into the preheated oven for 15-20 minutes or until the ingredients begin to simmer.

Reduce the oven temperature to gas mark 3/160°C/325°F/Aga simmering oven and continue to simmer for a further 10-15 minutes, or until you are ready to serve.

Dish up the steaks, sausages and tomatoes onto individual plates, or one large serving dish.

Boil the remaining liquid until it reduces and thickens before pouring it over the ingredients.

LAZY COOK TIPS

'Feather' steak used to be one of the cheaper cuts but as it has become more popular, the price has risen dramatically. Even so, it has a delicious flavour and should be enjoyed.

I prefer to buy it in one piece and slice to the required thickness. The residue scraped from the base of the pan is an important ingredient and adds flavour; do not discard it.

Allow the cooked casserole to rest in a fridge for a day or two before serving. This will improve the taste.

Should there be any ingredients remaining, use them to form the base of a soup by processing or liquidising the solid ingredients and heating with added extra stock – delicious!

DAUBE (BEEF CASSEROLE)

To be prepared a day before cooking.

Serves 6-8

900 g (2 lb) of lean stewing steak (cut into bite-sized pieces)
2 medium-sized onions (skinned and thinly sliced)
225 g (8 oz) carrots (scrubbed and thinly sliced)
2 garlic cloves (crushed)
2 dried bay leaves (crumbled)
2 teaspoons of dried oregano (or mixed herbs)
Freshly ground black pepper
300 ml (10 fl oz) of wine (red or white)
2 tablespoons of olive oil
225 g (8 oz) of rindless streaky bacon (cut into pieces)
225 g (8 oz) of mushrooms (wiped and sliced)
1 x 400 g tin of chopped tomatoes
A pinch of sugar
50 g (2 oz) of plain flour
600 ml (1 pint) of stock

TO PREPARE:

Put the meat, onions, carrots, garlic, bay leaves, mixed herbs, pepper, wine and oil and bacon into a bowl and stir well. Cover and leave in a fridge or cold larder to marinate for 24 hours, stirring occasionally.

TO COOK:

Layer the marinated ingredients (drained from the juices), with the mushrooms, tomatoes and sugar, into a large casserole dish, ending with the marinated ingredients on top. Mix the flour to a paste with a little cold water. Add this, along with the stock, to the marinated juices and stir over a gentle heat until it boils. Pour this over the casserole ingredients, cover and put into a hot oven (gas mark 6/200°C/400°F/Aga roasting oven) for 10 minutes or until it begins to simmer, then lower the temperature (gas mark 3/160°C/325°F/Aga simmering oven) and cook for 2-3 hours or until the meat is tender. Serve hot or cold.

FILLET STEAK WITH AN ARTICHOKE & APRICOT COMPOTE

Serves 4

4 fillet steaks (cut to a chosen thickness)
1 tablespoon of olive oil
25 g (1 oz) of butter
2 tablespoons of brandy
1 jar of sliced artichokes in oil
8 ready-to-eat dried apricots
½ teaspoon of fresh thyme leaves or ¼ teaspoon dried

QUICK FIX

Dry the steaks on kitchen roll and brush one side of each with oil.

Heat a large frying or sauté pan, add the butter and, when sizzling, add the prepared steaks and time the cooking according to whether you like them rare, medium or well done (see Lazy Cook Tips). Oil the upper side before turning and remove when cooked to time.

Prepare the compote by draining the artichokes from the oil, chopping them up roughly and adding to the apricots.

Add the brandy to the pan, scrape up any residue from the base and heat until boiling. Add the prepared compote, reduce the heat and stir until hot, seasoning at the end with thyme leaves.

Dish up the steaks on warmed individual plates. Stir any drained juices into the compote and stir before serving alongside the steaks.

Serve with new potatoes and a mixed green salad for a delicious summer meal. In the winter, you may like to accompany the steak with oven chips or jacket potatoes and a green vegetable.

LAZY COOK TIPS

Recommended cooking times: Rare — 2 minutes on each side, medium rare — 3 minutes, well done — 5 minutes.

Ripe, fresh apricots can be used in summer. I also recommend whole artichokes, bought by weight from a delicatessen.

STEAK, KIDNEY & MUSHROOM PIE

Prepare the following ingredients, except the pastry, a day before the pie is to be served.

Serves 6-8

700 g (1½ lb) of stewing steak (cut into bite-sized pieces)
225 g (8 oz) of ox kidney
2 tablespoons of plain flour seasoned with freshly ground black pepper
½ teaspoon of Marmite
2 dried bay leaves
450 g (1 lb) of mushrooms (wiped on damp kitchen roll)
1 teaspoon of mushroom ketchup
1 tablespoon of plain flour for thickening (optional)
225 g (8oz) of shortcrust or wholemeal pastry (see p30)

Set the oven to gas mark 6/200°C/400°F/ Aga roasting oven.

Remove the fat and core, then cut the kidney into small pieces.

Lightly coat the steak and kidney in seasoned flour, then transfer to an ovenproof casserole dish with the bay leaves.

Stir the Marmite into 300 ml (10 fl oz) of boiling water and pour over the casserole ingredients.

Stir, cover and cook in the preheated oven for 10-15 minutes, or until beginning to simmer.

Reduce the temperature (gas mark 3/160°C/325°F/Aga simmering oven) and cook until the meat is tender (this could take up to 2 hours).

Towards the end of cooking, slice and stir in the mushrooms and mushroom ketchup.

Blend 1 tablespoon of plain flour with a little cold water into a smooth paste and stir into the casserole. Cover and continue cooking for 20-30 minutes.

Remove the lid from the cooked ingredients and allow them to cool before storing, covered, in a fridge or cold larder, ready to make into a pie (see opposite).

TO MAKE INTO A PIE:

Set the oven to gas mark 6/200°C/400°F/ Aga roasting oven.

Remove and discard any fat from the surface of the casserole.

Place a pie funnel (or egg cup) in the centre of a deep pie dish and, using a slotted spoon, put the casserole ingredients in and around it, with some of the sauce.

Roll the pastry to 5 mm (¼ inch) thick, oil the rim of the dish and cover with strips of pastry.

Moisten with water before completely covering the ingredients.

Press down on the pastry rim and cut away the surplus, then seal the layers together by knocking against the edges with a knife.

Cut an X over the pie funnel, place in a baking tin and bake in the preheated oven for 30-40 minutes, or until the pastry has cooked and the ingredients are hot and bubbling.

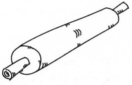

LAZY COOK TIPS

Once the pastry has cooked, you may need to reduce the oven temperature and bake for a little longer until the pie ingredients are hot (this is especially so if you are covering cold ingredients).

If you wish to decorate the pastry top before baking, cut 4 leaf shapes from the leftover pastry and arrange these around the X in the centre.

Moisten them with water to make them stick in place. Heat the remaining gravy and serve this separately.

Always popular, this makes an excellent meal to pack and serve on the first night of a self-catering holiday. Take the cooked ingredients in a sealed polythene bag and make into a pie as directed.

Stew & Dumplings

When he was a child this was our son William's favourite dish. It is a hearty family meal and sure to fill up even the hungriest of tums.

Serves 6
700 g (1½ lb) thick slices of shin or leg of beef
50 g (2 oz) of plain flour seasoned with freshly ground black pepper
50 g (2 oz) of beef dripping (or 2 tablespoons of olive oil)
450 g (1 lb) of onions (skinned and sliced into rings)
1 bay leaf
1 litre (1¾ pints) of hot water or stock
Dumplings (see opposite)

Set the oven at gas mark 3/160°C/325°F/ Aga simmering oven.

Heat half of the dripping or oil in a large saucepan.

Dry the meat on kitchen roll and cut into small pieces before lightly coating in the seasoned flour.

Add to the hot fat to brown all over, then remove from pan.

Scrape up any residue from the base of the pan, add the remaining dripping or oil and, when hot, add the prepared onion rings.

Stir well and sprinkle with the remaining seasoned flour.

Cover the pan and cook for 2 minutes, stirring occasionally.

Return the meat, the bay leaf and hot water or stock, stir, bring to boil and then reduce to a gentle simmer (occasional bubbles).

Cover the pan and continue simmering in the preheated oven for 1½-2 hours or until the meat is tender.

Drop the dumplings into the simmering stew.

Replace the lid and continue cooking for 30 minutes without lifting the lid, then serve.

Serve straight from the pan or put onto a heated serving dish. Sprinkle with freshly chopped parsley and surround with boiled potatoes and carrots.

DUMPLINGS

These are what I call 'real' dumplings and there is nothing to beat them. I am often so disappointed when a restaurant menu quotes 'and dumplings' but when they arrive they are not made as in this recipe – shame!

Makes 8-12
100 g (4 oz) of plain flour
1 heaped teaspoon of baking powder
Freshly ground white pepper
50 g (2 oz) of shredded beef suet
Cold water to mix

Mix all of the dry ingredients together in a basin using a blunt knife, then blend to a sticky paste under a cold running tap.

Place the mixture onto a lightly floured board and cut into 8 or 12 pieces. Shape each of the pieces into a ball using the palm of your hands (which should also be lightly floured).

Add to a gently simmering stew and cook for 30 minutes without lifting the lid.

LAZY COOK TIPS

There will be too much meat to brown all at one time; brown it in several batches adding a little more dripping or oil as is necessary. Thick slices of shin of beef (or leg of beef as it is now often sold) are, I believe, the only meat with which to make stew and dumplings.

The flavour is excellent and the string of gristle running through the meat adds a rich glutinous texture. This recipe can be completely cooked on a cooker hob – cover and keep at a gentle simmer (occasional bubbles) until the meat is tender before adding the dumplings. My late mother-in-law taught me that the secret to making dumplings light in texture is not to lift the lid once they have been added and to allow 30 minutes for them to cook to perfection.

Ox Cheek

I am so delighted that many of the cheaper cuts of meat that might have been cooked by my mother and others of her generation are now coming onto the market and are being recognised not only for their value for money but for their superior flavour and simplicity of cooking. Most need little more than gentle simmering for a few hours in wine and herbs.

Serves 2-3
1 ox cheek
Red wine (about half a bottle)
A collection of fresh mixed herbs (or a teaspoon of mixed dried)
1 dried bay leaf

Set the oven to gas mark 3/160°C/325°F/ Aga simmering oven.

Wipe the ox cheek with damp kitchen roll. Place in a small casserole dish, cover with wine and add the herbs (if they are fresh, tie them together with string).

Bring to a simmer over a gentle heat. Cover and transfer to the preheated oven to cook slowly for 2-3 hours or until the meat, when pierced with a metal skewer, is tender.

To serve, remove the meat and herbs from the pan, boil the liquid until it reduces considerably and begins to thicken. Slice the meat and pour the thickened juices over and around — delicious!

Lazy Cook tips

The reduction of the liquid will take several minutes, but watch from time to time because once it starts to thicken it all happens very quickly and you might be left with no more than a teaspoon of what is now a precious sauce. After the initial slow cooking this can be stored, when cold, in a fridge or cold larder for a few days and reheated to serve.

Minced Beef

1 large onion (skinned and chopped)
450 g (1 lb) of lean minced beef
1 x 400 g tin of chopped tomatoes
A pinch of sugar
50 ml (2 oz) of red wine (optional)
1 tablespoon of mixed fresh herbs, chopped (or ½ teaspoon of dried)
Freshly ground black pepper
A few shakes of Worcestershire sauce
Garlic (optional)
100 g (4 oz) of mushrooms (wiped and chopped)

Take a large frying or sauté pan and cover the base with water.

Bring to the boil, then add the prepared onion. Cover and cook until the onion begins to soften (approximately 2 minutes), adding a little more hot water if necessary to prevent sticking.

Add the minced beef and cook over a gentle heat for 5-10 minutes, breaking it down with a fork and stirring from time to time. Stir in the remaining ingredients, cover, and simmer for 15-20 minutes, or until the contents have blended together.

Serve hot from the pan, or leave to become cold and store, covered, in a fridge. Use within 4 days, removing all fat — which will have risen to the top — before reheating and serving.

Lazy Cook Tips

Minced beef is an extremely useful ingredient to have in store and will help to make a meal in minutes.

I recommend softening the onion in water (or stock) to reduce the fat content of the finished dish. Change the flavour by adding some chopped bacon and a teaspoon of mustard, chopped celery, nuts, olives or anything that takes your fancy.

Minced lamb or pork can also be cooked following this method. If cooking by Aga, the final simmering process should be done in the simmering oven.

MINCED MEAT STICK

This recipe is very popular with children and adults alike and will stretch a few ingredients to serve plenty.

Serves 4-6
450 g (1 lb) of cooked minced beef (see p125)
1 French stick/baguette or a similarly shaped loaf
Garlic cloves (several crushed)
1 x 200 g packet of potato crisps
50 g (2 oz) of grated cheese

QUICK
FIX

Set the oven to gas mark 6/200°C/400°F/ Aga roasting oven.

Slice the top from the loaf and tear the bread from the base to form a deep cavity.

Season with crushed garlic and fill with hot, cooked minced beef.

Top with the crisps crushed by hand into small pieces and sprinkle with grated cheese.

Place on a baking tray and cook in the preheated oven for 10-15 minutes.

Cut into chunks to serve.

LAZY COOK TIPS

The mince can be cooked a day or two in advance and stored, covered, in a fridge.

Remove and discard any fat which will have risen to the top and reheat the mince before adding to the loaf.

If the loaf is packed with hot ingredients, it can be simply finished off under a grill.

Make breadcrumbs with the remaining bread, dry them at a low temperature, then store in a jar for future use (see p223).

Osso Buco (Veal Shin Bones)

Serves 4
6 pieces of shin of veal
1 tablespoon of plain flour seasoned with fresh or dried sage
1 tablespoon of olive oil
425 ml (15 fl oz) of meat stock
1 dried bay leaf
Several stalks of fresh rosemary and sage (tied together)
2 teaspoons of redcurrant jelly
2 teaspoons of Dijon mustard

Set oven at gas mark 3/160°C/325°F/Aga simmering oven.

Heat the oil in a casserole or sauté pan with a lid. Dry the veal on kitchen roll before lightly coating in the seasoned flour.

Add to the hot oil and cook for a few minutes or until browned all over.

Add the meat stock, bring to a simmer and skim the top before adding the bay leaf and tied herbs.

Cover and cook in the preheated oven for 2 hours or until the meat is tender – test with a skewer. Put the pieces of meat onto a plate and, using a fork, remove all the meat from the bones and put into a hot serving dish. Cover to keep warm, discard the bones and all excess fat.

Remove the bay leaf and tied herbs from the pan, whisk in the redcurrant jelly and mustard and boil until it begins to thicken, then pour over the meat and serve.

Lazy Cook tips

Shin of veal is usually sold as osso buco. It resembles oxtail but is more meaty and paler in colour. The reduction of the meat juices can take a few minutes but be patient; it is worth the wait. This is a fine example of simple cooking using a cheaper cut of meat. Take advantage of this before increased sales result in increased prices!

Veal & Bacon Parcels with a Sun-dried Tomato Sauce

Makes 8

1 x 340 g packet (12 oz) of minced or ground veal

1 dessertspoon of olive oil

1 teaspoon of Dijon mustard

1 teaspoon of dried sage

1 egg yolk

1-2 tablespoons of fresh brown or white breadcrumbs

Freshly ground white pepper

16 slices of rindless back bacon (unsmoked)

2 teaspoons of sun-dried tomato purée

150 ml (5 fl oz) of stock

A pinch of sugar

Set the oven at gas mark 6/200°C/400°Φ/ Aga roasting oven.

Heat the olive oil in a shallow cast-iron pan. Add the veal and cook whilst breaking it down with a fork.

Stir in the mustard and sage. Remove from the heat and allow it to cool a little before stirring in the egg yolk and enough breadcrumbs to create a sticky consistency.

For each parcel cross 2 slices of bacon in the centre and pile the meat at the intersection.

Make into a parcel by covering with the bacon ends, finishing with a lean end.

Return to the pan, loose ends down, brush the top of each with oil and sprinkle with dried sage.

Bake in the preheated oven for 10-15 minutes or until the bacon has cooked.

Remove from the oven and put the parcels onto a hot serving dish and keep warm.

TO MAKE THE SAUCE:

Skim any excess fat from the pan, then whisk in 2 teaspoons of sun-dried tomato purée and a good pinch of sugar.

Add 150 ml (5 fl oz) of stock and a little freshly ground white pepper and allow it to simmer for a few minutes.

Pour a little of this sauce around the parcels and serve the remainder separately.

LAZY COOK TIPS

This recipe is best made in a pan that can be put from the hob into the oven — I find this type of pan invaluable and suggest you invest in one.

The parcels are remarkably quick to make and look so pretty when cooked. They are also quite filling; allow one per person, plus a few spares.

I serve them hot with leeks and rice, or cold cut into slices and arranged on individual serving plates.

I garnish with pickled cucumbers cut into fan shapes, a small bunch of red seedless grapes and a few salad leaves.

Serve the sauce separately.

PORK FILLET WITH SUN-DRIED TOMATOES & BLACK OLIVES

Serves 4

1 large pork fillet (dried on kitchen roll)
A little flour seasoned with freshly ground pepper
Oil from the sun-dried tomatoes
2 shallots (skinned and finely chopped)
150 ml (5 fl oz) of white wine
150 ml (5 fl oz) of meat or vegetable stock
1 teaspoon of sun-dried tomato purée
280 g jar of sun-dried tomatoes in oil (drained from the oil)
75 g (3 oz) of pitted dry black olives
A pinch of sugar

Set the oven to gas mark 6/200°C/400°F/ Aga roasting oven.

Trim the fillet of any excess fat or gristle before slicing thinly. Heat the oil in a large frying or sauté pan and lightly coat the fillet slices in seasoned flour. Add to the pan and brown for 1-2 minutes on each side, then put into a shallow ovenproof dish. Scrape any residue from the base of the pan, pour in a little water and add the shallots.

Cover and cook until softened, then add the wine and stock and boil to reduce a little. Stir in the tomato purée, the sun-dried tomatoes (drained from the oil on kitchen roll) and the olives. Season with a pinch of sugar and a little freshly ground pepper before pouring over the pork slices. Cover and bake for 10 minutes in the preheated oven. Then reduce the temperature to gas mark 3/160°C/325°F/Aga simmering oven and bake for a further 30 minutes, or until the pork is tender.

LAZY COOK TIPS

This recipe can be prepared a day or two in advance and reheated to serve. Store, covered, in a fridge or cold larder (please refer to reheating guidelines on p107). The combined flavours are excellent and the colours highly attractive. The remaining sun-dried tomato oil can be used for other recipes where oil is required.

PORK COOKED IN A PIQUANT SAUCE

Serves 4

4 spare rib pork steaks

1 tablespoon of plain flour

1 tablespoon of freshly chopped sage leaves (or 1 teaspoon of dried sage)

Freshly ground black pepper

1 tablespoon of olive oil

1 medium-sized onion (skinned and chopped)

1 teaspoon of sun-dried tomato purée or paste

1 tablespoon of Worcestershire sauce

1 tablespoon of cider vinegar

1 teaspoon of Dijon mustard

1 tablespoon of fresh lemon juice

1 tablespoon of demerara sugar

300 ml (10 fl oz) of stock or red wine (or a mixture of both)

Set the oven to gas mark 3/160°C/325°F/ Aga simmering oven.

Trim all excess fat from the steaks and dry them on kitchen roll.

Heat the oil in a sauté pan. Mix the sage and pepper into the flour and lightly coat each steak. Add the steaks to the hot oil and cook for about a minute on each side or until beginning to brown, then remove from pan.

Add a film of hot water to the pan and scrape up the residue from the base, before adding the prepared onion. Cover and cook until it begins to soften (approximately 1 minute). Stir in the remaining ingredients, then add the steaks and bring to a simmer. Cover and cook in the preheated oven for 30-40 minutes, or until the steaks are tender (test with a metal skewer). Serve onto hot plates or place along the centre of a hot serving dish. Boil the sauce to reduce and thicken before pouring it over the steaks.

Serve with rice and a vegetable of your choice.

LAZY COOK TIPS

This recipe can be completely cooked on a hob. Cover and keep at a gentle simmer (occasional bubble) until the steaks are tender.

PORK STEAKS WITH AN ORANGE & GINGER SAUCE

Serves 4

4 spare rib pork steaks

1 tablespoon of plain flour seasoned with freshly ground black pepper

1 tablespoon of olive oil

1 small onion (skinned and finely chopped)

150 ml (5 fl oz) of white wine

150 ml (5 fl oz) of concentrated orange juice

1 teaspoon of grated root ginger (or shavings)

1 tablespoon of double cream

Set the oven to gas mark 3/160°C/325°F/ Aga simmering oven.

Heat the oil in a sauté or large pan. Dry the steaks on kitchen roll, remove all fat and lightly coat in the seasoned flour. Add them to the hot oil and cook for about a minute on each side or until beginning to brown, then remove from pan.

Add a little hot water to the pan, scrape up any residue from the base and add the prepared onion, cover and cook until it begins to soften (about 1 minute), then remove from pan.

Add the wine and orange juice and boil over a high heat, uncovered, to reduce by half. Stir in the ginger and return the steaks and onion to the pan with any juices. Bring to a simmer, cover and cook in the preheated oven for 30-40 minutes or until the steaks are tender (test with a metal skewer).

Remove from the oven and put the steaks onto individual hot plates or a hot serving dish. Stir the cream into the pan juices and bring to a simmer. Pour a little over the steaks and serve the remainder separately. Serve with vegetables of your choice.

LAZY COOK TIPS

I use spare rib steaks for this recipe, although it is equally delicious made with slices of pork fillet. It can be prepared in advance and when cool, covered and stored in a fridge or cold larder. Serve within 3 days. Reheat to simmering before serving.

PORK STEAKS WITH AUTUMN FRUITS

A colourful meal with excellent flavours.
Take advantage of 'food for free' picked from the hedgerows.

Serves 4
1 tablespoon of olive oil
4 pork spare rib steaks
1 tablespoon of plain flour seasoned with a teaspoon of chopped sage
(fresh or dried)
150 ml (5 fl oz) of wine (red or white)
12-16 cherry tomatoes (washed)
A good handful of fresh blackberries (washed)

Heat the oil in a large frying or sauté pan. Dry the steaks on kitchen roll, trim off any excess fat, then lightly coat each in the seasoned flour. Add to the hot fat and cook on each side until they begin to brown. Remove from the pan.

Add the wine to the pan and as it heats scrape up any residue from the base and boil the wine for a minute.

Return the steaks, add the whole tomatoes and blackberries and bring to a simmer.

Cover and simmer for 30-45 minutes or until the steaks are tender (test with a metal skewer).

Serve the steaks on individual hot plates, or one large dish. Arrange the tomatoes and blackberries on and around.

Boil the remaining sauce until it begins to thicken, then spoon it on and around the steaks.

LAZY COOK TIPS

The juices from the steaks, tomatoes and fruits will make the sauce.
So quick and simple to prepare.

PORK BELLY SLICES WITH A MUSTARD PICKLE SAUCE

Serves 8 slices
1 kg (2 lb 4 oz) joint of pork belly
1 large jar of piccalilli or mustard pickle
2 tablespoons of milk

Set the oven at gas mark 6/200°C/400°F/Aga roasting oven.

Put the joint on a trivet in a roasting tin. Pour a little hot water into the tin and place in the preheated oven and roast for 45 minutes.

Reduce the oven temperature to gas mark 3/160°C/325°F/Aga simmering oven and continue cooking for a further 1½ hours. Remove from the oven and leave to rest for 20 minutes.

Remove the elastic which will have held the joint together during cooking. Cut off and keep all the top rind.

Slice the joint into 8 or more thick slices. Heat a large non-stick frying pan, add the slices and brown quickly on each side. Place onto hot individual serving plates or one large dish.

Wipe the base of the pan with kitchen roll, add the contents of the jar of piccalilli or mustard pickle to the pan with 2 tablespoons of milk, stir and boil before serving with the pork slices.

LAZY COOK TIPS

Pork belly is another of the cheaper cuts with excellent flavour. The removed rind can be made crisp (if not already so) by putting in a hot oven or under a grill. Serve this, broken into pieces, with the pork slices.

The mustard sauce is an excellent accompaniment to the meat; use home-made piccalilli if you have it. The juices from the pan in which the joint was cooked should be poured into a container and, when cold, stored in a fridge or cold larder. Remove all surface fat and use in soups, sauces and other meat recipes. Use within 3 days or freeze.

GAMMON STEAKS COOKED IN A TOMATO SAUCE

Serves 4
4 gammon steaks
1 tablespoon of olive oil
1 large onion (skinned and chopped)
1 x 400 g tin of chopped tomatoes
A good pinch of sugar
1 teaspoon of sun-dried tomato purée or paste
1 tablespoon of mixed fresh herbs (or ½ teaspoon of dried herbes de Provence)
Freshly ground black pepper
Fresh basil (or parsley)

Remove and discard all excess fat from the steaks. Heat the oil in a sauté or large pan, add the steaks and cook for a minute or two on each side to brown a little, then remove.

Add a little water to the pan and scrape up any residue from the base. Add the prepared onion and soften in the covered pan. Stir in all remaining ingredients and bring to a simmer, then return the steaks and spoon over the sauce. Cover and simmer gently for 10-15 minutes.

Serve directly from the pan or place the steaks down the centre of a hot serving dish, spoon the sauce on top and garnish with torn fresh basil leaves or chopped parsley. Serve with a vegetable of your choice, rice, pasta or couscous.

LAZY COOK TIPS

To make a richer sauce, add wine or cream (or both) before adding the gammon. Large gammon steaks can be cut into 2 portions, or broken into pieces to make them go further. In the past I have demonstrated this recipe to students, illustrating the speed, the simplicity and the minimum amount of cooking equipment required.

HAM & LEEK PIE

Serves 6-8
2 large leeks
Freshly grated nutmeg
450 g (1 lb) of cooked ham cut into bite-sized pieces
1 x 295 g tin of condensed chicken soup
300 ml (10 fl oz) of milk
150 ml (5 fl oz) of stock from the cooked leeks
225 g (8 oz) wholemeal or shortcrust pastry
(either bought or homemade – see p29)

Set oven at gas mark 6/200°C/400°F/Aga roasting oven.

Top and tail the leeks and cut into roughly 1 cm (½ inch) rings (including the dark-green stem). Rinse thoroughly in a colander under cold running water.

Bring to the boil 300 ml (10 fl oz) of water in a large pan. Add the leeks, cover and boil for 2 minutes. Strain and reserve the cooking liquid.

Place the leeks in a shallow ovenproof dish and grate nutmeg over them before topping with the ham pieces. Empty the soup into the pan, add the milk and reserved leek stock and stir together before pouring over the ham.

Roll the pastry to a size just slightly bigger than the dish, place on top and press the overhanging pastry into the sides. Use a knife to slash the pastry top several times.

Place the dish on a baking tray and bake in a preset oven for 20-30 minutes, or until the pastry is beginning to brown. Cover loosely with foil and bake for a further 10 minutes before removing from the oven and serving. Serve straight from the dish with vegetables of your choice.

LAZY COOK TIPS

Use the empty soup tin to measure the milk and stock – one tin measures 300 ml (10 fl oz). This pie makes good use of leftovers or end pieces of cooked ham. Alternatively, end pieces or thick slices are often available at reduced prices from deli counters and are ideal for this recipe. The liquid remaining from the cooked leeks should provide the amount of stock required in the recipe.

HAM & BEEF HASH

Serves 4
1 large onion (skinned and chopped)
2 teaspoons of tomato purée
2 teaspoons of Dijon mustard
150 ml (5 fl oz) of water
225 g (8 oz) of cooked ham (cut into small pieces)
225 g (8 oz) of corned beef (broken into small pieces)
1 tablespoon of raisins

QUICK FIX

Heat a little water in a medium-sized casserole dish or pan with a lid.

Add the onion, cover and cook for a few minutes until it begins to soften.

Add the tomato purée and mustard and mix to a sauce with the water.

Add the remaining ingredients, stir and bring to a simmer over a gentle heat before serving.

LAZY COOK TIPS

Corned beef is another of my favourite ingredients and mixes well with ham, which can often be purchased in pieces from a delicatessen or cold-meat counter at reduced prices and this is ideal for this recipe.

You can use any stock drained from cooked vegetables instead of water.

HAM WITH A
BLACK CHERRY SAUCE

Serves 4-6
700 g (1 ½ lb) joint of ham or bacon
2 dried bay leaves
10 whole black peppercorns
5 whole cloves
1 tablespoon of demerara sugar
Black cherry sauce (see opposite)

Put the joint into a large pan and cover it with cold water.

Place it over a gentle heat and bring slowly to a gentle simmer (occasional bubbles), without the lid on the pan.

Skim the top, then add the bay leaves, peppercorns, cloves and sugar. Cover and simmer gently for 30 minutes.

To serve hot, remove the joint from the pan, slice and put onto a hot serving dish.

Spoon over a little of the sauce, including a few cherries, and serve the remainder separately.

Store any remaining, covered, in a fridge or cold larder.

BLACK CHERRY SAUCE

100 ml (4 fl oz) of red vermouth (Martini Rosso)
50 ml (2 fl oz) of stock (preferably from the cooked ham or bacon joint)
2 tablespoons of redcurrant jelly
2 tablespoons of double cream
Several pinches of dried tarragon
425 g tin of pitted black cherries (drained from the juices)

Pour the Martini into a small pan and bring to the boil. Whisk in the redcurrant jelly and when dissolved add all the remaining ingredients.

Bring to a simmer and serve.

LAZY COOK TIPS

If time allows, put the joint to soak for an hour or two in cold water before cooking, strain off the water and cook as directed in the recipe.

The initial simmering process can take up to an hour but it is important to do this slowly to allow the heat to penetrate through the joint.

If cooking by Aga the final simmering process can be done in the simmering oven.

The remaining liquid (stock) can be used in soups and sauces.

To do this, remove and discard the bay leaves, peppercorns and cloves, and when cold, skim any fat from the top and discard. Then freeze the cold stock in polythene bags.

A joint of cooked ham or bacon is a most useful ingredient to have in store and can speed up the preparation of many meals.

BANGERS & MASH
WITH A PICKLE TOPPING

Add sparkle to this ever popular recipe while cutting down on preparation and washing up – highly recommended by the laziest of cooks!

Serves 4

12 sausages

700 g (1½ lb) of potatoes (peeled and chopped into small pieces)

50 g (2 oz) of butter

1 tablespoon of milk

Freshly grated nutmeg

1 large jar of pickled red cabbage

Set the oven at gas mark 6/200°C/400°F/ Aga roasting oven.

Place the sausages in a lightly oiled baking tray and bake in the preheated oven for 15-20 minutes, or until cooked.

Boil the prepared potatoes until they are soft.

Strain off the cooking liquid, add the butter, a tablespoon of milk and freshly grated nutmeg and mash them together until they are creamy and smooth – add more butter or milk if necessary.

Pour the cabbage and vinegar from the jar into a pan and heat.

To serve, pile the mashed potato onto individual hot serving plates, topping each of them with three cooked sausages and the pickled red cabbage, including a little of its accompanying vinegar.

LAZY COOK TIPS

The sausages can be cooked under a grill.

A little milk added to the potatoes will help to cut down on the fat content.

Pickled red cabbage adds flavour, colour and a crunchy texture to the traditional Bangers and Mash – it is also quicker than making gravy!

LAMB FILLETS WITH A GARLIC CREAM SAUCE

Serves 4
4 lamb fillets
A little olive oil
Garlic cream sauce – recipe below

Set the oven at gas mark 6/200°C/400°F/ Aga roasting oven.

Brush the base of an ovenproof dish with oil, add the fillets and cook in the preheated oven for 10-15 minutes.

To serve, cut each fillet into slices and arrange on individual hot serving plates. Drizzle with a little of the sauce and serve the remainder separately.

GARLIC CREAM SAUCE

1 large packet of Boursin garlic cream cheese
1 tablespoon of milk

Put the cheese and milk into a saucepan and whisk over a gentle heat until smooth. Serve hot or cold.

LAZY COOK TIPS

The length of cooking time will depend on the size of the fillets and whether you prefer them cooked pink or well done. I like to serve this with new potatoes and mangetouts. It is one of the quickest meals I prepare and quite delicious.

CROWN OF LAMB SERVED WITH A RED WINE & PESTO SAUCE

This is another recipe I have resurrected from my very early days of cooking. Although, as the title suggests, this is quite a majestic looking dish, it is actually one of the easiest of dinner party recipes. I served this to friends before leaving London to be married. It was a memorable and noisy party, not least the entry of the Crown of Lamb.

Serves 6
1 crown of lamb (prepared by a butcher)
1 bunch of watercress
Cutlet frills (one for each cutlet)
300 ml (10 fl oz) of red wine
1 tablespoon of pesto
1 tablespoon of redcurrant jelly

Set the oven to gas mark 6/200°C/400°F / Aga roasting oven.

Weigh the crown and allow 15 minutes per 450 g (1 lb) to serve pink, or 20 minutes per 450 g (1 lb) to serve well done. Stand the crown on a trivet in a meat tin and add about 300 ml (10 fl oz) of hot water. Place in the preheated oven and roast for around 10 minutes, then reduce the oven temperature (gas mark 4/180°C/350°F/ Aga baking oven) for the remainder of the roasting time.

Remove from the oven, place on a hot serving dish and keep warm. Spoon any excess fat from the pan juices before adding the wine and boiling for a few minutes to reduce. Whisk in the pesto and redcurrant jelly and bring to a simmer.

To serve, place a cutlet frill on each cutlet and fill the centre cavity with fresh watercress. Serve the sauce separately.

LAZY COOK TIPS

I recommend 2 cutlets per person and, as such, you may find 2 crowns are needed.

DEVILLED LAMB

Serves 4

4 fillets of lamb (dried on kitchen roll)
50 ml (2 fl oz) of double cream
50 ml (2 fl oz) of sour cream
2 tablespoons of Worcestershire sauce
1 tablespoon of sun-dried tomato purée
1 teaspoon of anchovy essence
½ teaspoon of dried mint
50 ml (2 fl oz) of wine (red or white)
Freshly ground pepper

Trim any excess fat from the fillets before cutting them into bite-sized pieces.

Mix all the remaining ingredients together, pour on top of the lamb, stir well and leave to marinate for 2-3 hours.

To cook, bring the marinated ingredients to a simmer over a gentle heat.

Cover the pan and simmer for 45 minutes to an hour or until the meat is tender. Serve hot or cold.

LAZY COOK TIPS

For a more concentrated flavour, allow the meat to marinate overnight.

If cooking by Aga, the simmering process should be done in the simmering oven.

LAMB'S LIVER

*I serve this with my own special vegetable and red wine gravy.
Overcooked liver is disgusting! Liver properly prepared and
cooked has the most delicate flavour, is highly nutritious and cheap.
If possible buy the liver in a piece, cut out and discard the area
containing tubes, then cut the liver into thin slices.*

Serves 4
700 g (1 ½ lb) of liver (sliced thinly)
2 tablespoons of plain flour seasoned with freshly ground black pepper
1 or 2 tablespoons of olive oil

Heat a tablespoon of olive oil in a large non-stick frying pan. Dry the liver
slices on kitchen roll. Lightly coat each slice in the seasoned flour and add to
the hot oil.

Cook until blood seeps out (about a minute), turn and cook for a further
minute.

Remove from pan and keep warm.

Continue until all the liver has been cooked, scraping the base of the pan
using a wooden spatula, and adding a little more oil if necessary.

LAZY COOK TIPS

*To make a really excellent meal I suggest the cooked liver is served
as follows:*

*Spread some mashed potato with Dijon mustard (see p170) onto
individual hot plates.*

*Top with 'The Humble Cabbage' (see p164), 2 or 3 slices of
cooked liver, and drizzle with red wine gravy (see opposite).*

RED WINE GRAVY

A rich gravy and especially good served with liver,
game and most red meats

300 ml (10 fl oz) of red wine
2 tablespoons of plain flour

Add a little hot water to the pan in which the liver was cooked and scrape up all the sediment.

Pour in 300 ml (10 fl oz) of red wine and bring to the boil. Mix 2 tablespoons of plain flour with cold water to make a smooth paste, then add to the red wine.

Boil until it thickens, stirring continuously, adding more water or wine until it is of a desired thickness.

LAZY COOK TIPS

For extra flavour use stock in place of water

Keep any leftover gravy to use another day or to add to a soup.

Once cooled, cover and store in a fridge or cold larder.

SPICY LAMB CASSEROLE

Serves 4

2 tablespoons of olive oil

450 g (1 lb) of diced lamb

25 g (1 oz) of plain flour

¼ teaspoon of mixed spice

Several good pinches of ground allspice

1 teaspoon of dried mint

1 large onion (skinned and roughly chopped)

50 ml (2 fl oz) of red wine

150 ml (5 fl oz) of stock

12 whole dried apricots (cut in half)

Set oven at gas mark 3/160°C/325°F/Aga simmering oven.

Heat 1 tablespoon of oil in a casserole or pan, dry the lamb on kitchen roll, toss in the flour and add to the hot oil.

Stir until it has browned, then remove from the pan.

Add 1 more tablespoon of oil to the pan and scrape up all residue from the base.

Add the prepared onion and scatter over any remaining flour, the mixed spice, ground allspice and mint.

Cover and cook until the onion begins to soften. Add the wine, stock and apricots, stir and bring to a simmer.

Cover and put into the preheated oven for 1 hour or until the meat is tender.

LAZY COOK TIPS

Lamb steaks or a boned half shoulder of lamb can be used in this recipe.

Venison Sausages Wrapped in Aubergine & Bacon with a Cranberry Sauce

Serves 4

4 venison sausages

4 thin slices of aubergine

4 thick rindless rashers of unsmoked bacon

100 ml (4 fl oz) of apple juice

100 ml (4 fl oz) of white wine

1 tablespoon of cranberry sauce

Set oven at gas mark 6/200°C/400°F/Aga roasting oven.

Wrap each sausage in a slice of aubergine, then a slice of bacon, and secure with a wooden cocktail stick.

Place these, loose bacon ends down, into a shallow cast-iron dish or roasting tin.

Pour over half the apple juice and bake in the preheated oven for 10 minutes.

Cover with foil and bake for a further 30 minutes, then remove from the pan and keep warm.

Add the remaining apple juice and wine to the pan juices and boil until they reduce and begin to thicken before stirring in the cranberry sauce.

Serve the sausages on hot individual plates or one large dish and spoon the sauce on and around.

LAZY COOK TIPS

If venison sausages are not available choose other gamey sausages.

Braised Venison

To be prepared 12-24 hours in advance of serving.
This is a great winter weekend recipe.

Serves 6-8

MAIN INGREDIENTS:

1½ kg (3½ lb) joint of venison (fillet, haunch, or any cut without bones)
2 tablespoons of plain flour seasoned with freshly ground black pepper
2 tablespoons of beef dripping or olive oil
1 tablespoon of redcurrant jelly
12 shallots (skinned and left whole)
12-16 pitted prunes

FOR THE MARINADE:

½ teaspoon of dried herbes de Provence
Freshly ground black pepper
2 good pinches of mixed spice
2 good pinches of ground cloves
2 dried bay leaves
1 lemon (cut into thick slices or quarters)
½ bottle of red wine

TO MARINATE:

Put the marinade ingredients into a large bowl or basin, add the joint and leave for 12-24 hours (in a fridge or cold larder), turning it every few hours.

To cook:

Drain the joint from the marinade (see Lazy Cook Tips). Heat the dripping or oil in a pan or casserole large enough to take all of the ingredients.

Dry the joint on kitchen roll and coat it in the seasoned flour before adding it to the hot fat and allowing it to brown all over (this may take 10-15 minutes).

Set the oven to gas mark 6/200°C/400°F/ Aga roasting oven. Remove the joint from the pan and mop up any remaining dripping or oil with kitchen roll.

Add hot water to cover the base and scrape up any residue. Add all the marinated ingredients and bring to the boil. Whisk in the redcurrant jelly and reduce to a simmer.

Return the joint and the prepared shallots to the pan, bring to a simmer, and then cover and place in the preheated oven for 10-15 minutes.

Reduce the oven temperature to gas mark 3/160°C/325°F/Aga simmering oven and cook for 1½-2 hours, or until the joint is tender, adding the prunes towards the end of cooking.

To finish off, remove the pan from the oven and place the joint onto a hot serving plate.

Remove the solid ingredients from the pan with a slotted spoon and arrange them around the joint. Discard the bay leaves.

Boil the remaining juices until they reduce and begin to thicken.

Pour a little of this juice over the joint, then serve the rest separately.

Slice to serve. This is a rich meal which I feel needs little more than boiled or jacket potatoes and a green vegetable served alongside it.

Lazy Cook Tips

To drain the marinated juices from the joint before browning, put it into a sieve over a bowl to catch all excess juices.

Do not flour the joint until the fat is hot. The length of cooking time depends on the quality of the joint: a cheaper cut will usually need longer to cook. It can also be made using a joint of beef. Use any remainders as the base for a soup.

SAVOURY MEAT BATTER

This is a popular family meal which will stretch a small quantity of mince to feed many.

Serves 6
300 ml (10 fl oz) of batter (see p263)
1 tablespoon of olive oil
1 medium-sized onion (skinned and chopped)
450 g (1 lb) of minced beef

Set the oven to gas mark 6/200°C/400°F/ Aga roasting oven.

Make the batter and leave to rest as directed in the recipe.

Heat 1 tablespoon of oil in a large, shallow, ovenproof dish or roasting tin in the preheated oven.

Add the prepared onion and mince, breaking it down with a fork, and return to the oven for 5-10 minutes.

Whisk 1 tablespoon of cold water into the batter mixture and pour it over the mince. Cook for 20-30 minutes, or until the batter has risen at the edges and is browning.

Serve straight from the oven, cut into wedges, with tomato ketchup or HP sauce and peas.

VILLAGE PIE

A really quick meal – especially popular with children.

Serves 6

1 large onion (skinned and chopped)
450 g (1 lb) of minced beef
225 g (8 oz) of chicken livers
1 x 400 g tin of chopped tomatoes
A pinch of sugar
50 ml (2 fl oz) of red or white wine, or stock
Freshly ground black pepper
Mixed herbs (fresh or dried)

TOPPING:
750 g packet of frozen oven chips

Set the oven to gas mark 6/200°C/400°F/ Aga roasting oven.

Cover the base of a large frying or sauté pan with water and, when boiling, add the chopped onion, cover, and cook for 1-2 minutes, or until the onion softens (add a little more hot water if necessary to prevent sticking). Add the minced beef, breaking it down with a fork, and cook over a gentle heat for 5-10 minutes, stirring from time to time. Stir in the remaining ingredients (except the oven chips), cover and simmer for 5-10 minutes, or until the contents have blended together.

Transfer the mixture to a large shallow ovenproof dish, top with oven chips and cook in the preheated oven for 20-30 minutes, or until the chips begin to brown and the ingredients are hot and bubbling.

Serve with vegetables of your choice; frozen peas and fresh carrots come highly recommended.

LAZY COOK TIPS

A good recipe to serve to a crowd – quickly! Prepare the ingredients in advance and store (covered) in a fridge or cold larder. Top with the chips and cook as directed in the recipe, allowing more time when reheating from cold.

SIMMERING OF MEATS

Perfect for feeding a crowd. This is an invaluable recipe for weekend entertaining when there seems to be a constant need for meals and very little time in which to prepare them — let alone relax and enjoy the weekend activities. This method of cooking ensures a succulent, juicy texture to the ingredients.

1½ kg (3½ lb) piece of ham or bacon
2 kg (4½ lb) whole chicken
900 g (2 lb) of sausages
A bunch of mixed fresh herbs (or a bouquet garni of dried herbs)
2 bay leaves
12 black peppercorns
12 whole cloves

Place all of the ingredients in a large casserole or pan and cover with cold water.

Slowly bring to a gentle simmer with the lid partially covering the pan — this should take at least 1 hour.

Skim the top, place the lid fully on the pan and continue gently simmering for 30 minutes.

Test that the cooking is complete by piercing the thickest part of the chicken leg with a skewer; the juices should run clear.

To serve hot:
1 tablespoon of tomato puree
A pinch of sugar
1 teaspoon of mixed, chopped, fresh herbs

Carve the ham and the chicken and arrange on a large, hot serving dish with the sausages, sliced diagonally.

Spoon some of the stock from the pan into a smaller pan, bring to a boil and whisk in a tablespoon of tomato purée, a pinch of sugar and some mixed chopped herbs. Pour a little over the meats and serve the remainder separately.

Serve with jacket potatoes and a green vegetable of your choice.

To serve cold:

Once the initial gentle simmering is achieved, remove the pan from the heat, cover completely with the lid and leave until cold, then store in a fridge or cold larder until needed.

Serve the carved cold slices on a large platter and scatter with watercress for instant eye-catching presentation.

Serve with salad, new potatoes and mayonnaise.

Lazy Cook Tips

A very large pan is required to hold all of the ingredients — a preserving pan can be used, using foil as a lid. It is very important that the initial simmering is done slowly in order for the heat to penetrate all the ingredients — the time will vary depending on the overall weight of the ingredients.

If cooking by Aga, once the initial simmering point is reached, continue the remaining simmering process in the simmering oven.

Use the stock for soups and sauces, store in a fridge or freezer. After the initial meal, the remaining ingredients can be used in other recipes: for example, 'Chicken with Apricots and Almonds', 'Spicy Chicken', 'Ham and Leek Pie' and many more. Refer to main index for recipe pages.

Chicken & Bacon Rolls with Sun-dried Tomatoes

Serves 4

4 chicken breasts

12 rashers of lean rindless streaky bacon

1 jar of sun-dried tomatoes preserved in oil

A few pinches of dried tarragon

150 ml (5 fl oz) of stock or wine

2 teaspoons of sun-dried tomato purée

Set the oven at gas mark 6/200°C/400°F/Aga roasting oven.

PREPARE EACH ROLL AS FOLLOWS:

Using 3 bacon rashers, stretch each with a knife before placing them slightly overlapping on a board or other surface. Top with 3 sun-dried tomatoes, a sprinkling of dried tarragon and a chicken breast, then roll in the bacon, like a sausage roll.

Smear the base of a shallow cast-iron pan with oil (from the jar of sun-dried tomatoes). Add the chicken rolls, placing the loose bacon ends down, and cook in the preheated oven for 10-15 minutes or until done; when pierced through the centre with a metal skewer the chicken juices should run clear. Transfer to a hot serving dish or individual plates.

Using a piece of kitchen roll, mop up any excess fat in the pan before adding the stock or wine and tomato purée to the pan juices. Stir together and boil until reduced and becoming syrupy. Pour over each chicken roll and serve.

LAZY COOK TIPS

This is another instance where a cast-iron pan, or a pan that can be used on a hob and in the oven, is invaluable for making the sauce using the meat juices. It is important that the chicken is thoroughly cooked and the time allowed will depend on the thickness of the chicken breast – adjust this as necessary.

CHICKEN BREASTS COOKED IN RED WINE & THYME

This recipe is cooked in a matter of minutes on a hob.

Serves 4
300 ml (10 fl oz) of red wine
300 ml (10 fl oz) of chicken stock
4 chicken breasts
Thyme (several sprigs fresh or ½ teaspoon of dried)
150 ml (5 fl oz) of single cream (optional)

Boil the wine and stock in a large pan, uncovered, for about a minute.

Add the chicken breasts and thyme and cook for 1 minute on each side.

Reduce the heat, cover and simmer for 5 minutes.

Cut into the thickest part of each breast, and if the inner flesh is pink, cook for a few minutes longer until the flesh is white and moist throughout.

To serve, remove and slice each breast and open like a fan onto hot individual serving plates.

Remove and discard the thyme stalks, add the cream to the pan juices and boil until they begin to thicken and reduce.

To finish, pour the sauce around each breast.

LAZY COOK TIPS

The cooking time will vary depending on the thickness and size of the breasts.

I cannot over-emphasise the importance of boiling all remaining liquid in the pan until it thickens. This will deepen the flavour and add finesse to the meal.

Another recipe to add excitement to your repertoire if cooking for one.

CHICKEN WITH APRICOTS & ALMONDS

A perfect recipe to make for a few, a crowd or for a fund-raising event. A Lazy Cook's alternative to coronation chicken!

Serves 6-8

450 g (I lb) of cooked chicken (broken into bite-sized pieces)

225 g (8 oz) of mushrooms (wiped and sliced)

100 g (4 oz) of dried apricots (cut into strips)

A good sprinkling of dried tarragon

250 g tin of Campbell's condensed mushroom soup

150 ml (5 fl oz) of white wine

150 ml (5 fl oz) of single cream

50 g (2 oz) of flaked almonds (browned)

Set the oven at gas mark 6/200°C/400°F/Aga roasting oven.

Layer the chicken, mushrooms and apricots in a shallow ovenproof dish and scatter with tarragon.

Heat the soup, wine and cream in a pan and stir until it begins to simmer. Pour over the chicken ingredients, scatter with the almonds and cover with foil.

Bake in the preheated oven for 20-30 minutes or until it is hot and bubbling.

LAZY COOK TIPS

This recipe can also be served cold. Cover the cooked ingredients and keep in a fridge or cold larder.

This is an excellent recipe if catering for lots of people. I have made it in vast quantities to serve at fund-raising events, assembling all the ingredients in huge casseroles, pans and even preserving pans.

Serve with rice (see p25) and mixed vegetables (frozen peas, diced carrots and celery).

From Plot to Pot

Over the years I have taken every opportunity to promote the use of seasonal ingredients and it pleases me that TV chefs and the media at large are now also doing so. The result is that many people are not only thinking 'seasonal' but are even contemplating growing their own vegetables.

Whether grown in a container or a growbag on a balcony, in a small garden, or harvested from an allotment, I guarantee the flavour will be such that you might almost think of becoming a vegetarian! The very thought of a freshly picked cucumber, or tomatoes, made into sandwiches to eat on a hot summer's day, or a dish of The Humble Cabbage or Quick Cauliflower Cheese served with a roast, excites my palate and gets my digestive juices flowing. Do try my vegetable recipes; the speed with which they can be prepared will give you more time to spend on the vegetable patch!

But if you are not into gardening, buy from your local farmer's market, farm shop or, if you are fortunate enough to have one, a good old-fashioned greengrocer.

From Plot to Pot

Ratatouille

Ratatouille Bake

Savoury Pumpkin Flan

Last-Minute Tomato Sauce

The Humble Cabbage Gets a Makeover

Vegetable Casserole

Baked Aubergine

Vegetable Bake (with Optional Bacon)

Baked Marrow

Mashed Potato with Dijon Mustard

Spicy Potato Mash

Celeriac & Parsnip Mash

Potato Gratinée

Quick Cauliflower Cheese

Beetroot

Spinach

Swiss Chard with Lemon Balm

Carrots Roasted with Dried Oregano

Bisley Beets

Marrow Rings with Spinach & Mushrooms

Vegetable Rice

GUIDELINES ON THE PREPARATION & COOKING OF VEGETABLES

Always remember, the preparation and cooking of vegetables is important and I pass on a few tips to guarantee that not a spoonful of these good flavours is poured down the drain!

With the exception of beetroots, most root vegetables only need scrubbing and topping and tailing prior to cooking and all uncooked trimmings and peelings put onto a compost heap.

To cook vegetables, choose a large saucepan with a fitted lid, even when cooking small quantities. Boil rapidly for 2-10 minutes in the minimum amount of water — top up with more water if necessary. When cooked to your liking, little more than a tablespoon of coloured liquid should remain — this is vegetable stock and is full of good flavours. Add it to gravy, soups or sauces, or store in a fridge and use the next day to cook more vegetables.

To save on power and washing-up, cook a variety of prepared vegetables together in one pot; for example carrots, cauliflower, mangetout and courgettes. Start with the carrots, which might need longer cooking, then add the cauliflower florets and finally, the mangetout and courgettes, which need little more than a minute cooking time.

Parboil vegetables for roasting for a minute or two to start the cooking process and heat the minimum amount of oil in the pan; you would be surprised at how little it takes to coat each vegetable. My motto is 'Add oil by the tablespoon — pour in wine from the bottle!'

I also believe to 'Waste not, want not'. Any remaining vegetables should be stored, covered, in a fridge to serve the next day. Stir into mayonnaise with fresh herbs for an instant 'Lazy Cook' salad, top with a little grated cheese and reheat in the oven or under a grill, or cut up and add to soup.

Ratatouille

Serves 4-6
1 large onion (skinned and sliced)
1 aubergine (topped, tailed and sliced)
1 green pepper (stalk and seeds removed, sliced)
1 x 400 g tin of chopped tomatoes
Garlic (optional)
Pinch of sugar
Freshly ground pepper
Several good pinches of mixed dried herbs

In a covered pan, soften the onion in a little boiling water.

Add all of the remaining ingredients, cover and simmer for 30-45 minutes, or until all of the vegetables have softened.

Serve as a vegetable accompaniment to meat or fish, or in a vegetarian recipe.

Lazy Cook Tips

To enrich the flavour, add a little red wine before simmering. Ratatouille is one of those really useful ingredients to have in store in winter.

It will keep (covered) in a fridge or cold larder for several days, or can be frozen.

Because of the protein content of the aubergine, it is extremely useful if catering for vegetarians, and it can be presented in so many different ways.

Any that remains will add flavour to a soup.

RATATOUILLE BAKE

Serves 6-8
225 g (8 oz) of self-raising flour
100 g (4 oz) of margarine (chopped into small pieces)
75 ml (2-3 fl oz) of milk
Ratatouille (see opposite)
100 g (4 oz) of strong cheddar cheese
50 g (2 oz) of walnuts (roughly chopped)
50 g (2 oz) of jumbo oats

Set the oven to gas mark 6/200°C/400°F/Aga roasting oven.

Blend the flour and margarine in a food processor for a few seconds. Slowly pour in the milk until a smooth dough is formed.

Roll out the dough to fit a large, lightly oiled, ovenproof plate or Swiss roll tin. Then cover it with the ratatouille, draining off any excess liquid.

Mix the cheese, walnuts and oats together and scatter generously over the top. Bake for 20-30 minutes. Slice to serve, hot or cold.

LAZY COOK TIPS

If this is baked in a Swiss roll tin, shape the dough up the sides of the tin to form a case in which to hold the filling. Tinned ratatouille can be used; just make sure to drain off any excess liquid before adding to the base. This liquid can be heated and served as a sauce, or added to soup.

SAVOURY PUMPKIN FLAN

Serves 6-8

450 g (1 lb) of pumpkin flesh (cut into small pieces)

1 medium-sized cooking apple

300 ml (10 fl oz) of water

Freshly ground white pepper

A good pinch of ground cloves

A good pinch of ground cinnamon

50 g (2 oz) of Gruyère cheese (grated)

1 tablespoon of cream (optional)

1 medium-sized onion (skinned and sliced into rings)

1 tablespoon of oil

1 ready-baked savoury pastry case

Set the oven to gas mark 6/200°C/400°F/Aga roasting oven.

Prepare the pumpkin by removing all of the seeds, centre pithy flesh and skin before weighing the required amount and cutting it into small pieces.

Skin, core and chop the apple.

Place the prepared pumpkin, apple and water into a pan and simmer (covered) until the pumpkin has softened, stirring occasionally and adding a little more water if necessary.

Remove from the heat and stir in the pepper, cloves, cinnamon, cheese and cream and put into the cooked pastry case.

Heat the oil in a pan and add the onion rings. Cover and cook until the rings begin to soften. Arrange over the pumpkin mixture in the flan case and bake in the preheated oven for about 10 minutes, or until the onions begin to brown. Serve hot.

LAZY COOK TIPS

Pumpkin absorbs a lot of water, so more may need to be added during the simmering process. When cooked it should resemble a purée texture. I serve this flan with crispy bacon and a Last-Minute Tomato Sauce (see opposite).

LAST-MINUTE TOMATO SAUCE

As the title suggests, this sauce can be made in no time at all and it is a wonderful speedy accompaniment to a variety of dishes.

6 tablespoons of tomato ketchup
1 teaspoon of Worcestershire sauce
A few dashes of Tabasco
1 teaspoon of fresh lemon juice
A good pinch of basil (fresh or dried)
A good pinch of sugar

Whisk all the ingredients in a pan and bring to a simmer, adjusting the seasonings to suit your palate.

Serve hot, warm or cold. Store in a covered container in a fridge or cold larder for future use. Use within 5 days.

LAZY COOK TIPS

Serve with or alongside any meal that needs a little extra moisture; add to pasta, rice or noodles, or even stretch a soup.

I find such ready-made sauces are invaluable, especially when time and resources are scarce.

THE HUMBLE CABBAGE GETS A MAKEOVER

Serves 6-8

1 large cabbage (preferably dark leaves)

25 g (1 oz) of butter

1-2 tablespoons of olive oil

1 large onion (skinned and sliced)

1 packet of smoked streaky bacon (cut into 3 cm/ 1 inch pieces)

1 ring of black pudding

(skinned and cut into slices approximately 1 cm/ ½ inch thick)

110 g packet of chorizo

(skinned and cut into slices approximately ½ cm/ ¼ inch thick)

1 large orange (zest and juice)

Slice the cabbage and wash under a cold running tap. Transfer it to a large saucepan containing approximately 300 ml (10 fl oz) of water. Cover and boil until the cabbage begins to soften (around 5 minutes), stirring from time to time. Add a little more boiling water if necessary to prevent burning.

Drain off all of the excess water. Return the pan to a gentle heat and stir in the butter to dry off any excess moisture. Then remove the cooked cabbage from the pan.

Heat the oil in the pan, add the prepared onion and bacon, cover and cook for a few minutes.

Meanwhile, prepare the black pudding and chorizo. Mix them into the onion mixture and cook until heated, stirring regularly. Add the cooked cabbage, orange juice and zest. Stir over a gentle heat until hot throughout before serving.

LAZY COOK TIPS

The water drained from the cabbage can be kept in a fridge to use when cooking other vegetables, or to add to soups, sauces and gravies. Use within 3 days.

This recipe is delicious and is especially good when served with calf's or lamb's liver.

VEGETABLE CASSEROLE

I find this a most useful vegetable recipe and I usually make enough to serve over several days. It is full of colour and good flavours.

Serves 6-8
2 tablespoons of olive oil
2 teaspoons of sun-dried tomato purée
2 large onions (skinned and sliced)
1 red, yellow and orange pepper (washed and sliced)
150 ml (5 fl oz) of water
Worcestershire sauce
1 teaspoon of runny honey
1 tablespoon of mushroom ketchup
6-8 large mushrooms (wiped and cut into quarters)
1 small packet of mangetout peas
1 small tin of sweetcorn
Freshly ground black pepper

Heat the oil in a large pan before adding the tomato purée and onion slices. Stir well, cover and cook over a medium heat for a few minutes.

Cut the peppers into strips and add to the pan along with approximately 150 ml (5 fl oz) of water, several good shakes of Worcestershire sauce, the honey and the mushroom ketchup. Bring to a simmer and cook (covered) until the peppers begin to soften. Stir in the mushrooms and mangetout and continue to cook (covered) until all the ingredients have cooked.

Immediately before serving, stir in the sweetcorn and season with freshly ground black pepper.

LAZY COOK TIPS

Remove and discard the stalk and core from the peppers beforehand. Include other vegetables as they come into season i.e. courgettes, French and runner beans etc. The flavours improve the longer it is kept – store in a fridge. Anything remaining can be processed or liquidised and made into soup. For a very quick meal, and very popular with vegetarians, simply serve it hot piled onto cooked noodles.

BAKED AUBERGINE

This is an excellent vegetarian recipe.

Serves 2
1 large aubergine
A little olive oil
1 medium-sized onion (skinned and chopped)
100 g (4 oz) of mushrooms (wiped with moist kitchen roll and chopped)
1 teaspoon of mushroom ketchup
1 teaspoon of sun-dried tomato paste
Freshly ground white pepper
4-6 sun-dried tomatoes preserved in oil (cut into strips)
Several good pinches of mixed dried herbs (or 1 teaspoon mixed fresh)
2 tablespoons of breadcrumbs (fresh or dried)
50 g (2 oz) of grated cheese

Set the oven to gas mark 6/200°C/400°F/Aga roasting oven.

Wash, top and tail the aubergine, and then cut in half lengthways.

Remove the flesh, keep it for later.

Score the flesh side of the aubergine, brushing this and the skin with oil before placing it, skin-side down, in a shallow ovenproof dish.

Bake in the preheated oven for 20-30 minutes, or until the skin has softened.

Meanwhile, prepare the filling by adding the chopped onion to a pan containing a little boiling water or stock.

Cover and cook until the onion begins to soften.

Cut the aubergine flesh into small cubes and add to the onion with the prepared mushrooms, mushroom ketchup, and sun-dried tomato paste.

Season with freshly ground pepper, stir, cover and cook for 2-3 minutes, or until the aubergine begins to soften (a little bit of vegetable stock or water may need to be added to prevent sticking).

Add the sun-dried tomatoes and herbs and stir.

Remove the aubergine cases from the oven and pack with the prepared filling.

Mix the breadcrumbs and cheese together and place on top.

Return to the oven and bake, uncovered, for 10-15 minutes, or until the topping is crisp and brown.

Serve hot with rice, fresh bread or salad.

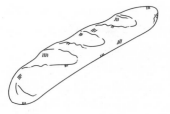

LAZY COOK TIPS

Oil from the jar of sun-dried tomatoes can be used.

I find that a grapefruit knife is a useful tool for removing aubergine flesh.

Nuts or dried apricots could also be added to the filling.

Aubergine has a good protein content so additional protein fillings (e.g. meat or poultry) should be kept to the minimum.

VEGETABLE BAKE
(WITH OPTIONAL BACON)

Serves 4-6

1 kg (2¼ lb) selection of parsnips, sweet potato and celeriac
1 large onion (skinned and chopped)
1 tablespoon of oil
175 g (6 oz) of grated cheese
150 ml (5 fl oz) of double cream (or a small carton of natural yoghurt)
Freshly ground white pepper
¼ teaspoon of medium curry powder
2 tablespoons of jumbo oats (or fresh breadcrumbs)
8 slices of lean rindless streaky bacon (optional)

Set the oven to gas mark 6/200°C/400°F/Aga roasting oven.

Peel the sweet potato and celeriac. Top, tail and scrub the parsnips and cut them all into small chunks. Boil in a pan of water until softened.

Heat the oil in a large frying or sauté pan. Add the prepared onion and, if being used, 5 rashers of the bacon (cut into small pieces). Cook until softened.

Strain the liquid from the cooked vegetables and mash together before adding to the cooked onion mixture.

Add 100 g (4 oz) of the grated cheese and the cream, season with pepper and curry powder and mix together. Lay out on a lightly oiled baking tray and shape like a cake approximately 25 cm (10 inches) in diameter. Press the remaining bacon rashers round the sides. Mix the remaining cheese with the oats and scatter on top.

Bake in the preheated oven for 20-30 minutes or until hot and bubbly. To serve, cut into slices and serve with fresh bread, rice or couscous.

LAZY COOK TIPS

If you prefer, you can cut all the bacon into small pieces and cook with the onion. It can be baked in a pie dish with the cheese and breadcrumb mixture on top. Use a mixture of cheeses, like Cheddar, Stilton and Double Gloucester, for good flavour and colour.

BAKED MARROW

A good filling recipe to feed to a crowd of hungry youngsters.

Serves 6-8
1 fat marrow
450 g (1 lb) of cooked minced beef (see p125)
4 large tomatoes
A sprinkling of granulated sugar
A little olive oil
A good handful of mixed fresh herbs (chopped) or a teaspoon of dried
Freshly ground black pepper

Set oven to gas mark 6/200°C/400°F/Aga roasting oven.

Wash the marrow, then cut in half lengthways and remove and discard the centre seeds and pith.

Score the marrow flesh and place, cut-side up, in a shallow ovenproof dish or roasting tin.

Fill the cavity with the cooked minced beef. Top with tomato slices brushed with oil and seasoned with a sprinkling of sugar, freshly ground pepper and chopped herbs.

Pour 600 ml (1 pt) of boiling water into the dish, cover with foil and bake in the preheated oven for 45 minutes to 1 hour or until the marrow is tender (test by piercing with a metal skewer).

Serve with fresh bread, rice, couscous or pasta.

VEGETABLE SIDE DISHES

MASHED POTATO WITH DIJON MUSTARD

700 g (1 ½ lb) of potatoes (scrubbed and chopped into small pieces)
2 tablespoons of milk
25 g (1 oz) of unsalted butter
Freshly grated nutmeg
2 teaspoons of Dijon mustard

Scrub the potatoes and cut into small chunks, put into a pan, cover with cold water, and boil until softened — test by piercing with a metal skewer.

Drain off and discard the cooking liquid. Add the butter, milk and Dijon mustard and mash until smooth.

SPICY POTATO MASH

Serves 4
700 g (1 ½ lb) of potatoes
2 tablespoons of milk
25 g (1 oz) of unsalted butter
½ a ring of black pudding (skin removed)

Scrub the potatoes and cut into small chunks. Put them in a pan, cover with cold water and boil until softened — test by piercing with a metal skewer.

Drain and discard the cooking liquid, then add the butter and milk and mash until smooth.

Crumble the black pudding in and stir. Serve hot.

LAZY COOK TIPS

When preparing potatoes for mashing, unless the potato skins are tough there is no need to remove them.

CELERIAC & PARSNIP MASH

Serves 4-6
450 g (1 lb) of parsnips
450 g (1 lb) of celeriac
Freshly grated nutmeg
1 tablespoon of single cream

Top and tail and scrub the parsnips before cutting into chunks. Peel the celeriac and cut into chunks.

Place both vegetables into a pan containing a little boiling water, cover and boil until softened – approximately 10 minutes. Drain off the cooking liquid (keep this for stock), season with freshly grated nutmeg and mash together. Stir in the cream and serve hot.

POTATO GRATINÉE

QUICK
FIX

Serves 4-6
900 g (2 lb) of potatoes
50 g (2 oz) of unsalted butter (melted)
Nutmeg (freshly grated)

Set oven to gas mark 6/200°C/400°F/Aga roasting oven.

Lightly oil a shallow ovenproof dish. Peel the potatoes, slice very thinly and layer into the prepared dish.

Pour melted butter over the top and season with freshly grated nutmeg. Bake in the preheated oven for 45 minutes or until the tops are browning and all the potato has softened – test by piercing a metal skewer into the centre. Serve hot from the oven.

LAZY COOK TIPS

Put the potatoes into the hot oven immediately to avoid the slices discolouring. Towards the end of cooking, the oven temperature can be reduced to gas mark 3/160°C/325°F/Aga simmering oven.

QUICK CAULIFLOWER CHEESE

QUICK FIX

Serves 4-6

1 cauliflower

175 g (6 oz) of grated cheese (a mixture of Stilton and Cheddar)

50 g (2 oz) of jumbo oat flakes

Set the oven to gas mark 6/200°C/400°F/Aga roasting oven.

Break the cauliflower into small florets, wash in a colander and place in a pan containing a little boiling water.

Cover, and boil for a minute or two to start the softening process.

Using a slotted spoon, transfer the cauliflower to a shallow ovenproof dish and add 3-4 tablespoons of the cooking liquid.

Mix the cheeses and oat flakes together and sprinkle over the cauliflower. Brown in the preheated oven for 10-15 minutes or under a hot grill.

LAZY COOK TIPS

Breadcrumbs can be used instead of oat flakes (see p223).

BEETROOT

Cut off the leafy tops to within 3 cm (1 inch) of the beetroot.

Put the beetroots into a pan and cover with cold water. Put the lid on the pan and simmer for an hour or longer (depending on the size of the beetroots).

Strain and discard the cooking liquid. Peel and slice the beetroots to serve, or as directed in a recipe.

LAZY COOK TIPS

Beetroots have a deliciously sweet flavour and I serve them in many ways.

Once cooked they can be stored, covered, in a fridge or cold larder; leave the skins on and use within 3 days.

The leafy tops, if in a fresh condition, can be cooked and have a similar flavour to spinach. Cook as you would spinach.

SPINACH

Wash a large quantity of spinach leaves (including the stalks if the spinach is young).

Drain well, then cook in a large pan over a gentle heat until the leaves have softened and wilted.

Remove from the heat and strain, keeping any juices.

Using scissors, cut up the cooked spinach, add a pat of butter and some freshly grated nutmeg. Stir over a gentle heat to dry off any moisture before serving.

LAZY COOK TIPS

Use frozen spinach if fresh is not available.

SWISS CHARD WITH LEMON BALM

Serves 4-6
900 g (2 lb) of Swiss chard
Fresh lemon balm leaves
1 lemon (juice and zest)

Wash the chard and cut the stalks from the leaves.

Cut the stalks into chunks and boil in a little water until softened but still crisp.

Remove from pan and lay onto the base of a shallow ovenproof dish.

Scatter with some lemon zest and a good squeeze of lemon juice.

Cover to keep warm.

Empty all but a smear of cooking liquid from the pan.

Add the leaves and cook over a gentle heat until softened and reduced (like spinach).

Cut up the leaves with scissors and spread them over the stalks.

Sprinkle with grated lemon zest and serve.

LAZY COOK TIPS

The remaining cooking water can be used for cooking other vegetables or to add to soups and sauces.

Store, when cold, in a fridge or cold larder and use within 2 days.

CARROTS ROASTED WITH DRIED OREGANO

If making this recipe using new young carrots, keep the tail and a fraction of the green leafy tops – I call these 'designer carrots'!

6 large carrots
1 tablespoon of olive oil
1 tablespoon of dried oregano

QUICK FIX

Set oven to gas mark 6/200°C/400°F/Aga roasting oven.

Scrub and top and tail the carrots, cut each in half lengthways, then put them in a pan containing a little boiling water.

Cover, and boil for a minute or two to start the softening process. Drain off the cooking liquid (keep this for stock).

Heat the oil in a shallow baking tin or ovenproof dish, add the carrots, scatter with oregano and stir to coat in oil.

Bake for 30-40 minutes or until the carrots have softened.

LAZY COOK TIPS

Oregano is a favourite herb of mine and one I grow all over the garden. Pick it as it flowers and dry in the oven on the lowest heat, including the flower heads. It has the most wonderful flavour.

Store in a jar and use regularly. Aga owners can dry herbs on the top surface.

BISLEY BEETS

Serves 4-6

4 large cooked beetroots (see p173)
1 large onion (skinned and sliced)
2 tablespoons of cider vinegar
1 tablespoon of demerara sugar
1 teaspoon of Dijon mustard
1 tablespoon of chutney

Set the oven to gas mark 6/200°C/400°F/Aga roasting oven.

Soften the onion in a little boiling water with the lid on the pan.

Skin and slice the beetroots and layer them into a shallow ovenproof dish.

Using a slotted spoon, strain the onion rings from the cooking liquid and layer on top of the beetroot slices.

Add all the remaining ingredients to the liquid in the pan, stir and bring to a simmer before pouring over the onion rings.

Cover with foil and heat in the preheated oven for 15-20 minutes or until hot throughout.

LAZY COOK TIPS

This recipe can be prepared in advance and stored, covered, in a fridge or cold larder.

Reheat as in the recipe but allow a little longer for all the ingredients to become hot.

Serve as a light meal with warm bread or rolls, or as a vegetable course with meat or fish.

MARROW RINGS WITH SPINACH & MUSHROOMS

Makes 6 rings
1 large marrow
450 g (1 lb) of cooked spinach (see p173)
Freshly grated nutmeg
6 large flat mushrooms (wiped)

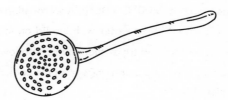

Set oven to gas mark 6/200°C/400°F/Aga roasting oven.

Slice the marrow into 6 rings, each approximately 3 cm (1 inch thick).

Remove and discard the centre pith and seeds before adding them to a pan of boiling water.

Boil for 1-2 minutes or until the marrow begins to soften. Using a slotted spoon, remove from the pan and place in a shallow ovenproof dish.

Fill each marrow cavity with cooked spinach, season with freshly grated nutmeg and top with a mushroom lightly brushed with olive oil.

Cover with foil and put into the preheated oven for 15-20 minutes or until the mushroom has softened.

Serve with salad for a light meal, or as a vegetable accompaniment to meat or fish.

VEGETABLE RICE

Perfect for feeding a crowd. I first served this to the bride, bridesmaids, family and close friends before we all walked to church for the wedding of our daughter, Nell.

30-40 servings
500 g packet of red Camargue rice (see p25)
500 g packet of short-grain wholemeal rice (see p25)
1 bunch of spring onions (sliced thinly, including the green leaves)
1 head of celery with leafy tops (cut into 1 cm (½ inch) slices)
6 roasted peppers (a mixture of colours) cut into strips
2 x 180 g jars of sun-dried tomatoes preserved in oil (cut into strips)
225 g (8 oz) of roasted cashew nuts
A selection of fresh herbs (chopped) or 1 teaspoon of mixed dried herbs
2 packets of mangetout peas (cooked and rinsed in cold water – leave whole)
2 tablespoons of oil from the sun-dried tomatoes

Mix all the prepared ingredients together and serve.

LAZY COOK TIPS

The rice can be cooked a couple of days in advance, put into large freezer bags and stored in the fridge.
For a buffet party serve this with cold chicken slices scattered with cress, and a green salad. Simple, but delicious.

SALADS

My grandmother's salads comprised of wet lettuce draining over an upturned saucer in a china bowl. My mother became really excited about salads following a holiday in France in the early Fifties. 'The lettuce is tossed in oil' she told us, but in those days, we didn't know what type of oil or where we could get it from – a chemist?

What would she make of the abundance of lettuce and other salad ingredients and the varieties of oils, vinegars and dressings available to us today. I do hope the handful of recipes I include in this section will introduce you to different varieties of 'salad' and you might become as excited by them as was my mother when she discovered 'dressed' lettuce for the first time.

SALAD RECIPES

Beetroot, Pear & Prawn Salad

Peas, Beans & Ham Salad

Red Chicory & Avocado Salad

Ham, Strawberries & Fresh Mint Salad

Vinaigrette

Mayonnaise

BEETROOT, PEAR & PRAWN SALAD

A salad to serve in autumn and winter
when beetroots and pears are plentiful.

Serves 4-6
2 large cooked peeled beetroots (see p173)
2 ripe pears (peeled and centre core removed)
100 g (4 oz) of cooked prawns
¼ teaspoon of dried tarragon
Vinaigrette (see p185)

Chop the beetroots and pears into similar sized chunks and put into a serving dish.

Add the prawns and tarragon and 2-3 tablespoons of vinaigrette and stir together.

Allow to rest for about an hour before serving.

LAZY COOK TIPS

This combination of flavours is lovely and delicate.

You can use fresh tarragon leaves but I find dried work just as well and are so convenient.

Peas, Beans & Ham Salad

6-8 servings

100 g (4 oz) of fresh or frozen peas

225 g (8 oz) of fresh or frozen broad beans

100 g (4 oz) of smoked ham (wafer-thin slices)

3-4 tablespoons of mayonnaise (recipe for home-made on p185)

A handful of mixed chopped fresh herbs (mint, sage and parsley)

Cook the peas and beans together in a little boiling water.

Strain into a sieve and rinse under a cold water tap and drain well before putting into a serving dish.

Remove and discard all fat from the ham.

Using scissors, cut the ham into ribbon strips and add to the peas and beans.

Add the herbs and mayonnaise and stir well before serving.

Lazy Cook Tips

For this recipe I use smoked Black Forest or Parma ham.

My crop of broad beans is more often than not a disaster and at the start of the season I unashamedly buy bags of early crop frozen broad beans

Red Chicory & Avocado Salad

This is a salad bursting with flavours and colour.

To serve 4-6
Assorted salad leaves
2 heads of red chicory
2 ripe avocado pears
4 spring onions (sliced thinly)
12 radishes (quartered)
1 carrot (grated)
Vinaigrette flavoured with honey

Cover a large platter with the salad leaves torn into pieces.

Cut the base from each chicory, pull off the leaves and arrange these in an outer circle on top of the salad leaves to resemble a flower.

Slice each avocado in half and remove the centre stone.

Slice each half into slices and arrange these inside the circle of chicory leaves.

Scatter the onions and radishes on top and finally add the grated carrot.

Stir ½-1 teaspoon of runny honey into some ready-made vinaigrette and pour over the salad or serve separately.

Lazy Cook Tips

This salad can be presented on one large platter or small individual plates.

Serve it with cold fish or poultry.

HAM, STRAWBERRIES & FRESH MINT SALAD

A delicious salad full of colour and good flavours and perfect for a light lunch on a hot summer day. Ideal served alongside home-made lemonade or Pimm's.

Mixed green lettuce leaves including rocket
Chopped celery
Vinaigrette
Fresh strawberries
Fresh garden mint
Cooked ham (thinly sliced)

Wash and spin dry the lettuce leaves, then pile them onto individual plates or into a large salad bowl.

Add the chopped celery, then drizzle with the vinaigrette and top with the ham slices (torn into strips) and strawberries (cut into halves or quarters if large).

Finally, scatter with chopped mint and serve.

LAZY COOK TIPS

If you should happen to have wild strawberries growing in the garden add these.

Parma or other thinly sliced smoked ham is also good with this recipe.

VINAIGRETTE

To two thirds good quality oil, add one third wine or cider vinegar and some freshly ground black pepper. Whisk all together.

LAZY COOK TIPS

I make up a quantity of this and keep it in a jar in readiness for use.

MAYONNAISE

There is nothing quite as delicious as home-made mayonnaise.

Makes about 300 ml (10 fl oz)
1 large egg
2 dessertspoons of wine vinegar
¼ teaspoon each of salt, ground white pepper, mustard powder
Sunflower oil (approximately 300 ml [10 fl oz])

Break the egg into a food processor or liquidiser and add the vinegar, salt, pepper and mustard powder.

Blend together for a few seconds before gradually pouring in the oil until the sauce thickens — the more oil that is added, the thicker it will become.

Store in a covered jar and keep in the fridge. Use within 7 days.

LAZY COOK TIPS

With the aid of a food processor or liquidiser, this can be made in minutes. I prefer to use sunflower oil, but others work just as well. Different flavoured vinegars can also be used. It is an extremely useful ingredient to have in store.

LAZY COOK NOTES

PUDDINGS

Pudding or dessert — call it what you will but I, like most people, cannot resist their temptation. Whether it is a humble rice pudding or a rich, creamy gateau, all my good intentions to lose a few pounds go out of the window — the diet can start tomorrow!

Having said that, our everyday puddings are mostly limited to fresh fruit and yoghurt, but when catering for the family and friends a pudding is a must. 'Hooray' says my husband!

Please note that I say a pudding. Yes, I usually offer just one pudding and follow this with a cheese course garnished with grapes or fresh fruit in season. I like to think that this is to provide a well-balanced meal, but you could be forgiven for saying it is because I'm too lazy!

Whether you offer just one sweet treat or a selection of puddings, I do hope you will feel tempted to make some of the recipes in this book, many of which can be made more quickly than you can grab a ready-made one from the supermarket shelf, and so much more delicious.

I am reminded of the little boy who, having returned home after a meal at a friend's house said to his mum '...and we had home-made pudding!' Go on, give the kids a treat!

PUDDING RECIPES

Apple Charlotte

Toffee Apple Pudding

Norwegian Apples

Apple Gateau

Bread Pudding with an Orange & Ginger Wine Sauce

Fresh Orange Jelly

Hot Orange Pudding

Mincemeat & Lemon Tart

Lemon & Lime Pots

Baked Summer Fruits Topped with Pink Meringue

Traditional Sherry Trifle

Raspberry Sponge

Sponge Drops & Fingers

Blackcurrant Crumble

Choux Pastry

Raspberry Buns

Pumpkin Pie

Banana Custard

PUDDING RECIPES CONTINUED

Fruit & Custard

Plum & Almond Pudding

Plums in Pimm's

Rhubarb Jelly with Strawberry Cream

Rhubarb & Ginger Crumble

Fruit Purée

Fresh Pineapple Rings with a Honey & Brandy Syrup

Meringue

Meringue Shapes & Toppings

Meringue Plates

Bramble Meringue Pie

Lemon Meringue Gateau

Lazy Lemon Meringue Pie

Coffee Meringue Gateau

Baked Chocolate Meringue Pots

Chocolate Bombe

Chocolate Squares

Chocolate Blancmange

APPLE CHARLOTTE

This is a delicious pudding and so quick to make.

Serves 6-8
700 g (1½ lb) of Bramley apples
75 g (3 oz) of shredded suet
75 g (3 oz) of demerara sugar
175 g (6 oz) of dried breadcrumbs (brown or white) – see p223
1 lemon (juice and zest)

Set the oven to gas mark 6/200°C/400°F/Aga roasting oven.

Peel, core and chop the apples.

Mix the suet, sugar, breadcrumbs and lemon zest together.

Lightly oil a deep pie dish and fill it with layers of apple and the breadcrumb mixture, starting with the apples and ending with the breadcrumbs.

Pour lemon juice over the top and bake for 20-30 minutes.

Serve hot with custard or cream.

LAZY COOK TIPS

The use of dried breadcrumbs gives this Charlotte a lightness of texture.

Add more lemon juice if you enjoy a really strong lemon flavour.

Serve from the pie dish onto a hot serving plate.

Loosen the sides with a palette knife before turning out.

Sieve the top with icing sugar and garnish with more lemon rind.

TOFFEE APPLE PUDDING

Serves 6-8
700 g (1½ lb) of Bramley cooking apples
225 g (8 oz) of dark cane caster sugar
225 g (8 oz) of self-raising flour
Several good pinches of ground cinnamon
100 g (4 oz) of butter
A little icing sugar

Set the oven to gas mark 4/180°C/350°F/Aga baking oven.

Line an 18 cm (7 inch) loose-based round cake tin with a baking parchment cake tin liner.

Peel, core and slice the apples into a large bowl and stir in the sugar.

Process the flour, cinnamon and butter until it is a pastry crumb texture, and stir this into the apples.

Pack the mixture into the prepared tin and bake for 45-60 minutes, or until golden on top.

Remove from the tin, place on a hot serving plate and peel off the outer lining paper. Cover the top with sieved icing sugar.

Serve hot, warm or cold with single cream, ice cream or custard.

LAZY COOK TIPS

The longer it is left to bake, the stickier and more toffee-like it becomes.

Reduce the oven temperature to suit your time schedule.

In the unlikely event there is any remaining, this is delicious served as a cake - ideal for a lunch box treat.

Norwegian Apples

The combination of flavours and textures makes this very simple pudding really special. I cannot take all the credit for this recipe, the idea for which was passed on to me by Evy who over many years has entertained us with so many very delicious meals.

Serves 4-6
1 kg (2¼ lb) of apple purée
300 ml (10 fl oz) of double cream
1 tablespoon of biscuit crumbs
75 g (3 oz) of dark chocolate (chopped into pieces)
75 g (3 oz) of walnuts (chopped into pieces)

Pile the apple purée onto a large serving dish.

Whip the cream to a soft peak and spread over the purée.

Mix the biscuit crumbs, chocolate and walnuts together, drizzle over the cream and serve.

Lazy Cook Tips

At the beginning of the cooking apple season keep a quantity of pureed apples in the fridge. In 'Mo'-ments you'll be able to prepare and present this delicious pudding to unexpected friends – or give the family an unexpected treat. So much quicker than making apple pie but equally delicious.

Apple Purée

Peel, quarter and remove the core from the Bramley apples before putting into a pan with a tablespoon of water added, cover and cook over a low heat until they turn into a pulp. For more details and other fruit purée recipes see p215.

Apple Gateau

We have two large Bramley apple trees in the garden, and when we first moved to Bear House I was overwhelmed by the autumn crop. This is one of the recipes I created at that time and passed on at the cookery demonstrations I gave in my kitchen. I am often reminded of it by those who still enjoy making it.

Serves 6-8
1 packet (24) sponge fingers or boudoir biscuits
450 g (1 lb) of apple purée (see opposite)
300 ml (10 fl oz) of double cream
Grated dark chocolate or chocolate squares (see p227)

Line the base and ends of a 900 g (2 lb) loaf tin with greaseproof paper or foil.

Fill the tin with layers of sponge fingers and apple purée, beginning and ending with sponge fingers.

Cover with a piece of card wrapped in foil and press with a light weight: leave overnight in a fridge or cold larder.

To serve, remove the weight and card, loosen the sides with a palette knife and turn onto a serving dish.

Cover with whipped cream and scatter with grated chocolate, or press Chocolate Squares (see p227) into the sides and ends and spike into the top.

Slice to serve.

Lazy Cook Tips

This is a light and delicious pudding which can be made two or three days in advance and stored in a fridge or cold larder.

Add the cream before serving.

BREAD PUDDING WITH AN ORANGE & GINGER WINE SAUCE

I remember well the bread pudding my mother used to make and which I loved. My recipe is, I think, equally delicious, but is much quicker to make. The ginger wine sauce makes it a very special pudding to serve on all occasions.

Serves 6
100 g (4 oz) of fresh breadcrumbs
100 ml (4 fl oz) of milk
1 dessertspoon of black treacle
1 tablespoon of marmalade
25 g (1 oz) of shredded suet
½ teaspoon of mixed spice
100 g (4 oz) of dried apricots (sliced)
Orange & Ginger Wine Sauce (see opposite)

Heat the milk and stir in the treacle until it has dissolved. Add all the remaining ingredients and stir well.

Pack into a lightly oiled pie dish and leave to rest for 15-30 minutes.

Sprinkle with a little demerara sugar and bake for 30-40 minutes (gas mark 4/180°C/350°F/Aga baking oven).

Serve hot or cold with Ginger Wine Sauce or custard.

LAZY COOK TIPS

This recipe can also be served as a cake – when cold cut it into wedges.

For a more eye-catching presentation, prepare it as follows. Smear butter over the base of a pie dish and cover with demerara sugar. Arrange the whole apricots on top before covering with the pudding mixture.

Bake as directed in the recipe, but to serve, turn it out onto a hot serving plate. Serve the Ginger Wine Sauce separately.

Orange & Ginger Wine Sauce

*I was first introduced to ginger wine by a dear friend and
neighbour, who one year invited me to help decorate the
church in readiness for the annual service of remembrance.
After the service I would return to her kitchen and enjoy a
glass of ginger wine. These memories return each autumn
and Christmas when a glass of ginger wine is a warm and
comforting treat on a frosty winter day. I could not resist
combining it with another favourite winter flavour - oranges,
and including them in my winter recipe development.*

1 fresh orange (grated zest and juice)
1 teaspoon of orange flower water (optional)
50 ml (2 fl oz) of ginger wine

Put all the ingredients together in a pan and simmer for a few minutes,
stirring constantly.

Serve at once or prepare in advance and reheat to serve.

Lazy Cook Tips

*This is a delicious sauce to serve with numerous puddings or ice-
creams. It can be stored in a covered container in a fridge or cold
larder.*

*Orange flower water is a useful ingredient to have in store and
can be added to many cake and pudding recipes as it has a very
delicate flavour.*

It can be bought from most delicatessens and some supermarkets.

Fresh Orange Jelly

300 ml (10 fl oz) of hot water
1 tablespoon of runny honey
25 g (1 oz) of gelatine crystals
4 large oranges (squeezed)
1 lemon (squeezed)

Pour a little hot water into a measuring jug, add the gelatine crystals and stir until dissolved.

Add the honey and make up to 300 ml (10 fl oz) with hot water and stir.

Leave to stand until cold before stirring in the fruit juices.

Taste for sweetness and add more honey or a little brown sugar if necessary.

Pour into one large or several small jelly moulds or ramekins and put into a fridge or cold larder until set.

Serving suggestions – with sponge drops, ice cream or single cream.

Lazy Cook Tips

Serve direct from the dish or remove from the mould by loosening the jelly using your fingertips.

Gently ease it out onto a serving dish. If it's being stubborn, stand the mould in very hot water for a few seconds before trying again.

HOT ORANGE PUDDING

Oranges are at their best in winter and this is an excellent way of making them into a delicious pudding.

Serves 4
4 tablespoons of orange marmalade
2 large oranges
1 packet of ready-rolled puff pastry
Single cream

QUICK FIX

Set the oven to gas mark 7/220°C /425°F/Aga roasting oven.

Spread the marmalade over the base of a shallow round pie dish.

Cut the oranges into thin slices (discard any pips) and arrange, overlapping, on top of the marmalade.

Lightly oil the rim of the dish and cover with pastry. Pressing down on the oiled rim, trim off all surplus pastry and prick the top lightly with a fork.

Stand the dish on a baking tray and bake for 20-30 minutes, or until the pastry has risen and is browning.

Remove from the oven and allow to cool slightly before turning onto a hot, deep, serving dish.

Serve hot or warm with single cream.

LAZY COOK TIPS

It is important to remember to take care when turning the pudding onto the serving dish because the marmalade is hot and runny.

The orange peel will soften during cooking and will add flavour to the pudding.

MINCEMEAT & LEMON TART

A tart made in mo-ments from store cupboard ingredients.
A fine example of Lazy cooking!

QUICK
FIX

Serves 6
1 ready-made sweet pastry case
1 jar of mincemeat
1 jar of lemon curd
1 fresh lemon
Breadcrumbs (dried or fresh — see p223)

Set oven to gas mark 4/180°C/350°F/Aga baking oven.

Put the pastry case on a baking tray and spread mincemeat over the base.

Squeeze the fresh lemon juice into the curd and spread on top of the mincemeat.

Top with breadcrumbs and bake in the preheated oven for 15-20 minutes.

Serve hot, warm or cold with single cream.

LAZY COOK TIPS

This is so much quicker than making individual mince pies and the addition of lemon curd complements the sweetness especially if bought mincemeat is used.

LEMON & LIME POTS

Make a day or two before serving.

Makes 4-6
1 packet of trifle sponges
1 jar of lemon curd
2 lemons (juice and zest)
1 lime (juice and zest)
50 g (2 oz) of icing sugar
150 ml (5 fl oz) of double cream

Split the trifle sponges, spread each half with lemon curd and put them into a large bowl.

Remove the zest from the lemons and lime and keep it in a pot covered with cling film.

Squeeze the juice from 1½ lemons and the whole lime and pour it over the sponges, then mash with a fork.

Spoon the mixture into 4 or 6 ramekins or small glass dishes and smooth the top.

Using the juice from the remaining half lemon make up a runny icing and pour this on top of each. Cover with cling film and store in a fridge.

To serve, pile lightly whipped cream on top and mark with a fork before scattering with lemon and lime zest.

LAZY COOK TIPS

The longer the sponges are allowed to soak before topping with cream the better the flavour.

After storing in the fridge bring them back to room temperature to serve.

BAKED SUMMER FRUITS TOPPED WITH PINK MERINGUE

This is a lovely pudding to make when the summer fruits are at their best.

Serves 6
2 peaches
2 nectarines
4 apricots
225 g (8 oz) of strawberries
225 g (8 oz) of raspberries

1 tablespoon of dark muscovado sugar
2 teaspoons of orange flower water
4 tablespoons of brandy
2 large eggs
100 g (4 oz) of caster sugar
A few spots of pink food colouring (optional)

Wash the fruits before preparing. For the peaches, nectarines and apricots, cut in half and remove the stone. For the berries, remove and discard the stalk.

Set the oven to gas mark 4/180°C/350°F/Aga baking oven.

Place the prepared fruits in a pie dish and sprinkle over the sugar, orange flower water and brandy. Make the meringue topping by whisking the egg whites and food colouring until they are stiff and dry (of a cotton wool consistency).

Add the sugar and whisk until it has been incorporated. Spread the mixture to completely cover the fruit, making sure the meringue is touching the rim of the dish.

Place it on a baking tray and bake in the preheated oven for 5-10 minutes, or until the meringue begins to brown.

Reduce the oven temperature (gas mark 3/160°C/325°F/Aga simmering oven) and continue baking for 20-30 minutes, or until you are ready to serve.

Traditional Sherry Trifle

Serves 8-10
900 ml (1½ pints) of whole milk
2 heaped dessertspoons of Bird's instant custard powder
1 dessertspoon of granulated sugar
A few drops of vanilla essence
1 packet of trifle sponges
Strawberry jam
300 ml (10 fl oz) of sweet sherry
410 g tin of strawberries
300 ml (10 fl oz) of double cream
Flaked almonds (lightly browned)
Glacé cherries

Mix the custard powder to a runny paste with a little of the milk. Warm the remaining milk before adding the custard powder mixture and sugar and stir until it boils and thickens a little.

Stir in the vanilla essence, remove from the heat and leave to cool a little.

Split the trifle sponges and spread each with strawberry jam and place in a large deep trifle dish.

Drizzle with sherry and mash with a fork. Add the strawberries, strained from the juices, cover with the custard and leave to set.

To serve, spread the top with lightly whipped cream and scatter with flaked almonds and glacé cherry halves.

Lazy Cook Tips

Sherry trifle is always a popular pudding. This is a recipe my mother would have used when eggs were too scarce to use in puddings.

Take care not to make the custard too thick as it will thicken as it cools.

I make trifle a day before it is needed and add the cream and decoration to serve.

RASPBERRY SPONGE

This is one of my favourite puddings using rounds of fatless sponges.

Serves 8

FOR THE FATLESS SPONGES:
3 large eggs
75 g (3 oz) of caster sugar
75 g (3 oz) of plain flour
A little extra caster sugar

FOR THE FILLING:
284 ml (10 fl oz) carton of double cream
225 g (8 oz) of fresh raspberries (washed)
Sifted icing sugar

TO MAKE THE FATLESS SPONGES:

Set the oven to gas mark 3/160°C/325°F/Aga simmering oven.

Place the eggs and sugar into a mixer bowl or basin and put into the oven for 2-3 minutes to warm.

Oil (or line with Bake-O-Glide) 2 baking trays. Weigh and sieve the flour.

Remove the bowl from the oven and increase the oven temperature to gas mark 6/200°C/400°F/Aga roasting oven.

Using an electric hand mixer, whisk the warmed ingredients at top speed until they are of a thick consistency (like spreading cream).

Sieve the flour again, then stir it into the egg mixture.

Spread onto the prepared trays into 2 round shapes approximately 25 cm (10 inches) each in diameter and sprinkle the tops with caster sugar.

Bake in the hot oven for 6-10 minutes, or until they turn a biscuit colour.

Remove and transfer immediately onto a wire cooling tray (use a large palette knife to ease the plates from the lining).

If you're not using immediately, wait until they've cooled, then store them in an airtight container or large polythene bag. Use within 1 week or freeze.

LAZY COOK TIPS

Warming the eggs and sugar in the oven is my Lazy Cook answer to whisking them in a bowl over hot water which seems to take an eternity. In the time saved you will be able to prepare other ingredients.

But do watch the ingredients carefully, the eggs must not cook! — you will be able to time this with practice.

When made this can also be shaped into sponge drops or fingers (see p204).

RASPBERRY FILLING:

Whip the cream to a soft, spreadable consistency and spread half over one sponge placed on a serving plate, sugar-side down. Top with the raspberries (reserving 3 or 4), spread the remaining cream on the underside of the second sponge and place over the raspberries.

Sift the icing sugar on the top and place the reserved raspberries in the centre with small sprigs of mint.

LAZY COOK TIPS

I often demonstrated the making of these rounds for this and other puddings and was invariably asked 'Why can we not use a fatless sponge cake cut into rounds?' The simple answer is 'You can, but the result would not produce the texture, flavour, or presentation required.' With practice, the sponges are very easily made and are a most useful confection to have in store. I very much doubt that you are able to buy anything resembling them. Experiment using other fillings.

Sponge Drops & Fingers

Excellent for toddlers and young children.

Makes approximately 24
2 large eggs
50 g (2 oz) caster sugar
50 g (2 oz) plain flour
A little extra caster sugar

Make up following the directions for fatless sponge on page 202.

Drop the mixture onto the prepared baking tray/s. Use the tip of a dessertspoon to shape into drops or from the side of a tablespoon to shape into fingers.

Sprinkle each with caster sugar and bake in the preheated oven for 4-5 minutes, or until they turn a pale biscuit colour.

Cool and store as directed in the main recipe.

Serve as biscuits alongside other puddings or sandwich together with cream, jam and fresh strawberries as a pudding.

Lazy Cook Tips

I often refer to these as 'visiting fingers' because they are perfect to take when visiting someone either in hospital or at home and in need of a little special treat.

BLACKCURRANT CRUMBLE

This is such an easy pudding and I often serve it after a Sunday roast.

Serves 6-8
680 g jar of blackcurrants in syrup
225 g (8 oz) of plain flour
100 g (4 oz) of butter (preferably unsalted)
75 g (3 oz) of demerara sugar

QUICK
FIX

Set the oven to gas mark 6/200°C/400°F/Aga roasting oven.

Spread all of the blackcurrants and about half of the syrup in a shallow ovenproof dish.

Process the flour and one tablespoon of sugar for a few seconds, add the butter (cut into pieces) and process until it is a pastry crumb texture.

Spread this over the blackcurrants and scatter the remaining sugar on top.

Stand the dish on a baking tray and bake in the preheated oven for 15-20 minutes or until hot and bubbly.

Serve hot or cold with the remaining syrup, single cream or ice-cream.

LAZY COOK TIPS

Make sure the blackcurrants are bottled in syrup.

If you spread the blackcurrants in the dish and have the crumble ingredients ready processed, then the crumble can be put together very quickly and baked in the oven while the main course is being eaten.

It may be necessary to reduce the oven temperature after 20 minutes to gas mark 4/180°C/350°F/Aga baking oven.

This is a really delicious pudding, one of my favourites.

CHOUX PASTRY

150 ml (5 fl oz) of cold water
50 g (2 oz) of butter
75 g (3 oz) of plain flour
2 large eggs

Set the oven to gas mark 6/200°C/400°F/Aga roasting oven.

Slowly heat the water and butter in a pan until the butter has melted. Increase the heat and when the liquid begins to rise, add the flour.

Beat until the mixture leaves the side of the pan, then remove from the heat and leave to cool a little. Add the eggs and beat until the mixture is smooth.

Lightly oil a baking tray and put tablespoons of the pastry on, spaced well apart. Bake in the preheated oven for 15-20 minutes or until they have puffed up and are crisp.

Remove from the oven and using a pointed knife, make a slit in each to allow steam to escape. Remove and discard all uncooked paste.

Serve immediately with fillings of your choice or freeze when cold.

LAZY COOK TIPS

Take great care when slitting the cooked choux as the hot steam escapes. Choux pastry is mostly associated with éclair or profiterole, but it has many other uses, savoury and sweet. It is a quick and easy pastry to make.

The mixture can be made and kept in a fridge for several hours before it is baked.

Always cook it in a hot oven and serve as soon as possible. After it has baked, it should be crisp and light in texture.

Cooked choux shapes can be frozen – as they begin to thaw, pop them into a hot oven for a few minutes to bring them back to a crisp texture.

RASPBERRY BUNS

Makes about 10
Choux pastry (see opposite)
300 ml (10 fl oz) of double cream
450 g (1 lb) of fresh raspberries
Icing sugar to sift

Drop spoonfuls of choux pastry onto a lightly oiled baking tray and bake as in the main recipe.

Fill the buns with whipped cream and raspberries and sieve with icing sugar.

Pile onto a large plate or dish and serve.

LAZY COOK TIPS

You can be adventurous with your choice of filling too.

Try it flavoured with coffee or melted chocolate – whatever your sweet tooth desires.

Make these smaller by dropping them from a teaspoon.

To make a savoury option, fill with cream cheese and freshly chopped parsley. Serve several as starters, or pile them on to a dish and serve as a party canapé.

For further help and ideas for making and storing choux pastry refer to notes under L/C tips on page 206.

Pumpkin Pie

Serves 6-10
450 g (1 lb) of pumpkin flesh (cut into bite-sized pieces)
1 medium-sized Bramley apple (peeled, cored and chopped)
1 x 450g (1 lb) jar of mincemeat
A good pinch of ground cloves
1 ready-baked sweet pastry case
2 large eggs
100 g (4 oz) of caster sugar
Several good pinches of mixed spice

Set the oven to gas mark 6/200°C/400°F/Aga roasting oven.

Prepare the pumpkin by removing all of the seeds, centre pithy flesh and skin, before weighing the required amount and cutting it into small pieces. Place in a pan with the apple and cover with cold water.

Simmer, covered, until the pumpkin has softened, stirring occasionally and adding a little more water if necessary.

Remove from the heat and stir in half a jar of mincemeat and the ground cloves and allow to cool a little before spooning it into the baked pastry case.

Make the meringue topping by whisking the egg whites until they are stiff and dry (of a cotton wool consistency), add the sugar and spice and whisk until it has been incorporated. Spread over the top of the pumpkin mixture and bake in the preheated oven for 10 minutes, or until the meringue begins to brown.

Serve warm or cold with single cream.

Lazy Cook Tips

Pumpkin absorbs a lot of water as it cooks, so add more as necessary; it should resemble a purée when cooked.

The oven temperature can be reduced (gas mark 3/160°C/325°F/ Aga simmering oven) once the meringue has browned.

BANANA CUSTARD

Real comfort food loved by children and adults alike.

Serves 4-6
4-6 bananas
600 ml (1 pint) of whole milk
2 dessertspoons of Bird's custard powder
1 tablespoon of granulated sugar
A few drops of vanilla extract (optional)
300 ml (10 fl oz) of whipping cream (optional)
1 tablespoon of dark grated chocolate

Half fill a serving or trifle dish with peeled, sliced bananas. Mix the custard powder to a smooth paste using a little of the cold milk.

Warm the remaining milk, then add the custard powder paste with the vanilla essence and sugar and stir until it boils and thickens.

Remove from the heat and allow it to cool a little before pouring over the bananas.

Allow to set before serving. Spread with whipped cream and grated chocolate or grated chocolate only.

LAZY COOK TIPS

This can look quite attractive made in individual glasses or dishes if you prefer.

Ready-grated chocolate is quick to use. I recommend you keep a tin in store.

FRUIT & CUSTARD

This is an example of my increasingly lazier recipes — what started life as Upside-Down Trifle is now reduced to plain, though equally delicious, Fruit & Custard!

Serves 6

600 ml (1 pint) of whole milk
1 dessertspoon of granulated sugar
¼ teaspoon of vanilla extract
4 large eggs (whisked together)
25 g (1 oz) butter (optional)
Freshly grated nutmeg (optional)
300 ml (10 fl oz) of double cream
225 g (8 oz) of fresh strawberries, raspberries or other summer fruits

Set the oven to gas mark 4/180°C/350°F/Aga baking oven.

Warm the milk, sugar and vanilla in a pan before pouring it onto the whisked eggs. Now pour the mixture through a sieve into a 900 ml (1½ pint) soufflé dish or 6 ramekin dishes.

Top with a little butter and freshly grated nutmeg.

Stand the dish(es) in a roasting tin and add warm water to come approximately halfway up.

Bake in the preheated oven for 10 minutes before reducing the temperature to gas mark 3/160°C/325°F/Aga simmering oven and cook until the custard has set.

Remove from the oven, lift out of the tin and leave until cold.

To serve, cover with whipped cream and top with whole strawberries, raspberries or any soft summer fruits.

LAZY COOK TIPS

The custard can be baked in advance, covered, and stored in a fridge or cold larder. Eat within 4 days.

To make the quantity of cream go further, add 2 tablespoons of milk during whipping.

PLUM & ALMOND PUDDING

Serves 6-8

50 g (2 oz) of plain flour

1 level teaspoon of baking powder

50 g (2 oz) of caster sugar

25 g (1 oz) of ground almonds

50 g (2 oz) of margarine (softened)

1 large egg

¼ teaspoon of almond essence

450 g (1 lb) of plums (wash, cut in half and remove stones)

1 dessertspoon of demerara sugar for topping

Set the oven to gas mark 4/180°C/350°F/Aga baking oven.

Oil a shallow loose-based cake tin, approximately 18 cm (7 inches) in diameter.

Blend the flour, sugar, baking powder and ground almonds in a food processor for a few seconds.

Add the margarine, egg and almond essence and process until smooth.

Spread into the prepared tin and cover with the plum halves (cut-side down).

Sprinkle with demerara sugar and bake in the preheated oven for 30-45 minutes, or until firm to the touch.

Serve hot or warm with cream, ice-cream or custard.

When cold, serve as a cake.

LAZY COOK TIPS

Stand the tin on a baking tray to bake in case the ingredients spill over.

Choose Victoria plums if available. The texture is slightly soggy and the flavours are excellent.

PLUMS IN PIMM'S

A grown-up jelly!

Serves 6
450 g (1 lb) of Victoria plums (washed, cut in half stones removed)
350 ml (12 fl oz) of water
1 sachet of gelatine (a scant ½ oz)
200 ml (8 fl oz) of Pimm's No. 1
1 tablespoon of runny honey

Spread the prepared plums in a glass dish.

Pour 50 ml (2 fl oz) of hot water into a measuring jug, sprinkle in the gelatine, and stir or whisk until dissolved.

Make up to 350 ml (12 fl oz) with hot water and stir in the honey.

Once this has dissolved, stir in the Pimm's and pour over the plums.

When cold, cover and put into a fridge or cold larder to set.

LAZY COOK TIPS

Leaf gelatine can also be used for this recipe — follow the manufacturer's directions to dissolve.

RHUBARB JELLY WITH STRAWBERRY CREAM

Serves 6

1 packet of raspberry-flavoured jelly cubes
2 serving spoons of cooked rhubarb and juice
150 ml (5 fl oz) of double cream
225 g (8 oz) of fresh strawberries (hulled and washed)

QUICK
FIX

Break the jelly cubes into a measuring jug.

Pour in up to 300 ml (10 fl oz) of boiling water and stir until the cubes have dissolved.

Stir in the cooked rhubarb and 2 large spoons of rhubarb juice: make up to 600 ml (1 pint) with more boiling water.

Pour into a mould or dish and leave to set.

For eye-catching presentation, spread the jelly with whipped cream and top with strawberries.

LAZY COOK TIPS

This jelly is packed with good fruit flavours, ideal for serving in summer.

It can be made using gelatine crystals or leaf gelatine – follow the manufacturer's instructions to make the jelly.

RHUBARB & GINGER CRUMBLE

QUICK FIX

Serves 6-8

700 g (1½ lb) of fresh rhubarb

225 g (8 oz) of plain flour

100 g (4 oz) of unsalted butter

100 g (4 oz) of demerara sugar

75 g (3 oz) of crystallised ginger (cut into small pieces)

Set the oven to gas mark 6/200°C/400°F/Aga roasting oven.

Cut off and discard the leafy end and the stalk from the rhubarb.

Cut each stick into roughy 2cm (1 inch) lengths. Wash in a colander under a cold running tap, and place in a large pie dish with 4 tablespoons of cold water.

Process the flour and butter to a pastry crumb texture, then add 75 g (3 oz) of the sugar, and the ginger. Blend for a few seconds to mix together.

Spread over the rhubarb and sprinkle the remaining sugar over the top.

Stand the dish on a baking tray and bake in the preheated oven for 20-30 minutes or until it begins to bubble around the edge and the rhubarb has softened — test with a skewer.

Serve straight from the oven.

LAZY COOK TIPS

Crumbles are one of my favourite ways of serving fresh fruit in all seasons, not least because they are so quick and easy to prepare.

There is no need to cook the chosen fruit before adding the prepared topping, be it fresh or direct from the freezer; it will soften as it cooks.

I do not recommend adding sugar to the fruit. The combination of sweet and sharp flavours result in a perfect crumble.

Fruit Purée

Especially good for serving to toddlers and young children.

When making for babies and young children, remove the skin and stones of large fruits: apples, pears, peaches, nectarines, apricots, plums, etc. Cook in bulk and sweeten to taste with runny honey or raw cane sugar. Cook the fruit in a little water until it is soft and liquidise or process to a purée, then rub through a sieve before serving to babies and very young children. When cold, cover and store in a fridge and use within 3 days. To freeze, pack the cold purée into freezer bags of varying sizes, label and date.

Apple

One of the easiest and most successful of purées. Peel, core and slice Bramley apples into a pan with just enough water to moisten the base. Add several whole cloves (optional), place the lid on the pan and cook over a gentle heat until the apples pulp and rise in the pan. Remove from the heat. Sweeten, then store or freeze as above.

Pear

Peel and discard the skin. Cut into quarters and remove centre core and pips. Follow instructions for cooking, sweetening and storing as above.

Peach, Nectarine, Apricot, Plum

Wash the whole fruit before cutting in half and discarding the stones. Slice or quarter and follow instructions for cooking, sweetening and storing as above.

Rhubarb

When the rhubarb is young there should be no need to remove the outer skin. Wash, top and tail each stick and cut into approximately 3 cm (1 inch) lengths. Follow instructions for cooking, sweetening and storing as above.

Fresh Pineapple Rings with a Honey & Brandy Syrup

I think of pineapple as a winter fruit and often serve it over the Christmas period. This is a refreshing pudding to serve following a rich meal.

Serves 4-6
1 large pineapple
1 teaspoon of runny honey
2 tablespoons of brandy
1 teaspoon of rose water (optional)

Prepare the pineapple by cutting off the top and end, stand it on one end and cut off and discard the spiky skin as close to the flesh as possible.

Remove and discard any bits which remain in the pineapple using the point of a knife or a potato peeler.

Turn the pineapple onto its side and slice to the desired thickness. Cut out the centre stalk from each ring (a small pastry cutter is ideal for this).

Put the rings into a serving dish.

To make the syrup, dissolve a teaspoon of runny honey in 50 ml (2 fl oz) of hot water, then stir in the brandy and rose water.

Allow to cool a little before pouring over the rings.

Serve with single cream or vanilla ice cream.

Lazy Cook Tips

I must emphasise the importance of the preparation of the pineapple. Make sure you remove the black bits remaining in the fruit after you have cut off the outer spiky skin.

These are as offensive to my palate as the outer inedible shell of apple pips resulting from badly prepared apples before cooking.

MERINGUE

BASIC INGREDIENTS:
50 g (2 oz) caster sugar to each large egg white

Experience has taught me that successful meringue making comes not from the age or the temperature of the eggs but from the whisking of the whites before sugar is added.

This should be stiff and dry and the texture of cotton wool – dense and pure white with no minute bubbles round the side of the bowl.

Then add the sugar, whisking continuously until the meringue is of a creamy texture.

Shape directly onto Bake-O-Glide or parchment covering a baking tray into rounds or rings of varying sizes, or into individual small or petite meringues dropped from a spoon.

Dry the meringue shapes in a low oven (from gas mark 3/160°C/325°F/ Aga simmering oven or lower) for several hours or overnight.

They are ready to remove when the lining peels away from the meringue.

When cold, store in airtight containers or polythene bags.

Meringue Shapes
Bases and Plates

Spread the meringue into round or rectangular shapes in the sizes required. A four-egg-white meringue mixture will shape 2 x 25cm (10 inches) in diameter round bases (see opposite).

Rings

Spread the meringue into rings of the size required leaving a centre cavity. A three-egg-white meringue mixture will shape 2 x 25 cm (10 inch) rings.

Small or Petite Meringues

Drop the meringue from a teaspoon, dessertspoon or tablespoon (depending on the size required) or shape through a piping bag. Dip in melted chocolate to serve or sandwich together with whipped cream.

Lazy Cook Tips

If a bubbling of liquid appears on the base of the meringue during drying this is because the sugar has not been completely folded into the egg whites. This will add a slightly toffee texture to the meringue. Cream will soften meringue making it easier to slice.

Meringue Toppings

When meringue is used as a topping for other ingredients, e.g. lemon meringue pie, they are usually placed in a hot oven (gas mark 6/200°C/400°F/Aga roasting oven) for 5-10 minutes or until they begin to brown, when they can be served.

If you require a crisper meringue reduce the oven temperature to gas mark 3/160°C/325°F/Aga simmering oven until ready to serve.

MERINGUE PLATES

To make 2 x 25 cm (10 inches) in diameter
4 large eggs (whites only)
225 g (8 oz) of caster sugar
A pinch of cream of tartare

Set the oven to gas mark 2/150°C/300°F/Aga simmering oven.

Cover two baking trays with household parchment or Bake-O-Glide.

Whisk the egg whites until they are stiff and dry (of a cotton wool texture with no tiny bubbles round the edge).

Whisk in the sugar and cream of tartare until the texture becomes creamy, then spread this mixture onto the prepared baking trays in rounded shapes, each approximately 25 cm (10 inches) in diameter.

Place in the preheated oven to dry (this can take between 2 and 4 hours).

Take them out of the oven and remove them from the paper. Store in airtight polythene or freezer bags until needed.

LAZY COOK TIPS

Make sure the whites are really stiff before the sugar is added. The plates are dry when the lining paper will peel easily from the meringue.

Meringues of all shapes and sizes are useful to have in store; they will remain crisp for at least 2 months.

The egg yolks can be cooked (drop into boiling water or bake in a low oven).

Cover and store in the fridge; use for crumbling into soups or onto salads. Use within 3 days.

Bramble Meringue Pie

An excellent pudding to make in the autumn when hopefully blackberries are available for the picking from hedgerows.

Serves 6-8

1 ready-baked pastry case

450 g (1 lb) of Bramley cooking apples (peeled, cored and sliced)

225 g (8 oz) of blackberries (washed)

Sugar to taste

2 egg whites

100 g (4 oz) of caster sugar

A few spots of pink food colouring (optional)

Set the oven to gas mark 6/200°C/400°F/Aga roasting oven.

Cook the apples and blackberries in a covered pan on a gentle heat, add sugar to taste and leave to cool while you make the meringue.

Add a few spots of food colouring to the egg whites and whisk until stiff and dry (of a cotton wool texture).

Add the sugar and whisk until it has been incorporated.

Fill the flan case with the cooked apple and blackberry mixture and cover with the meringue.

Bake in the preheated oven until the meringue begins to brown.

Serve warm or cold with single cream.

Lazy Cook Tips

The flavours of this pudding are excellent. It can be baked in the hot oven and when the meringue begins to brown, the temperature can be reduced to gas mark 3/160°C/325°F/Aga simmering oven to allow the meringue to become crispy.

As a Lazy Cook I always keep a store of ready-baked flan cases; these are available from most delicatessens or supermarkets.

With such ingredients to hand, this pudding can be made in minutes.

LEMON MERINGUE GATEAU

Assembled in Mo-ments! – a Lazy Cook favourite.

Serves 8-10
2 meringue plates (see p219)
1 jar of lemon curd
1 lemon (juice and zest)
300 ml (10 fl oz) of double cream

Stir a tablespoon of lemon juice into 4 tablespoons of lemon curd.

Spread this over the base of a meringue plate, and then spread with half of the whipped cream.

Top with the second meringue plate, then spread with the remaining cream.

Heat a tablespoon of lemon curd in a small pan until it becomes runny.

Using a teaspoon, trail this in lines across the cream, then scatter with lemon zest.

Leave in a fridge or cold larder for several hours before serving.

LAZY COOK TIPS

I assemble this pudding directly onto a serving plate, securing the base meringue with a tablespoon of whipped cream.

If the cream is accidently overwhipped, very gently stir in a tablespoon or two of milk and it should return to a smooth consistency.

This pudding is best made several hours before it is served.

LAZY LEMON MERINGUE PIE

Deliciously lazy!

Serves 6-8
1 ready-baked sweet pastry case
1 x 411 g jar of lemon curd
2 lemons (juice and zest)
75 g (3 oz) of dried breadcrumbs (see opposite)
2 large eggs
100 g (4 oz) of caster sugar
A few spots of yellow food colouring (optional)

Set the oven to gas mark 4/180°C/350°F/Aga baking oven.

Place the pastry case on a baking tray.

Empty the lemon curd into a bowl, then add the juice and zest of both lemons and the breadcrumbs. Stir together before spreading into the pastry case.

Make the meringue topping by whisking the egg whites and the food colouring until they are stiff and dry (of a cotton wool consistency).

Add the sugar and whisk until it has been mixed in well, then spread this to cover the lemon filling, touching the edge of the pastry case.

Bake in the preheated oven for 5-10 minutes (or until the meringue begins to brown), then reduce the temperature (gas mark 3/160°C/325°F/Aga simmering oven).

Continue to bake for 30 minutes, or until you wish to serve the pie.

Serve warm with single cream or ice cream.

DRIED BREADCRUMBS

Blend pieces of bread in a food processor or liquidiser until of a breadcrumb texture.

Place on a tin tray and dry until crisp in a cool oven or on top of an Aga. Store in jars.

LAZY COOK TIPS

I recommend at least 4 tablespoons of lemon juice is added to the lemon curd. If the lemons are not very juicy more than 2 may be needed.

Remove the zest from the lemons before squeezing. Dried breadcrumbs will give the filling a lightness in texture.

Ready-baked pastry cases are available from supermarkets and delicatessens. I find them an invaluable store cupboard ingredient for sweet or savoury fillings.

Coffee Meringue Gateau

I have often served this meringue at fund-raising parties and I can guarantee that after such events the telephone is hot with requests for the recipe. Meringue plates cost pence to make but pounds to buy — have a go!

Serves 8-10 slices
2 meringue plates (25 cm/10 inch in diameter — see p219)
2 teaspoons of instant coffee granules
1 tablespoon of hot water (almost boiling)
300 ml (10 fl oz) of double cream
2 tablespoons of single cream
1 tablespoon of ready-grated chocolate

Dissolve the coffee in the water and allow it to cool a little.

Pour all the cream and coffee into a large bowl and whip to a soft peak.

Sandwich the meringue plates together on a large serving plate or a silver cake board using half the cream and spread the remainder on top.

Cover with grated chocolate.

Lazy Cook Tips

Assemble this pudding several hours before serving, this will enable the cream to soften the meringue and make it easier to cut.

If the cream is overwhipped, gently stir in a little milk to bring it back to the required consistency.

Put a spoon of cream on the plate before adding the meringue to keep it firmly in place.

Baked Chocolate Meringue Pots

Makes 4
1 Terry's dark chocolate orange
4 teaspoons of Cointreau, brandy or chocolate liqueur (optional)
3 egg whites
175 g (6 oz) of caster sugar

QUICK
FIX

Set the oven to gas mark 6/200°C/400°F/Aga roasting oven.

Divide the chocolate segments evenly between 4 ramekin pots and pour a teaspoon of your chosen liqueur on top.

To make the meringue topping, whisk the egg whites until they are stiff and dry (of a cotton wool texture), add the sugar and whisk until it has been incorporated and is of a creamy texture.

Spoon the mixture onto each ramekin, piling it above the rim.

Place on a baking tray and put into the preheated oven for about 2 minutes, or until it begins to brown on top.

Reduce the temperature to gas mark 3/160°C/325°F/Aga simmering oven and leave for 30 minutes, or until you are ready to serve them directly from the oven.

Lazy Cook Tips

This is a quick and most delicious pudding; the melted chocolate beneath the soft meringue is so very good.

Should there be any remaining pots, store them in a fridge and reheat for a few minutes to serve.

Chocolate Bombe

Serves 6-8
To be prepared and frozen:
300 ml (10 fl oz) of double cream
175 g (6 oz) of dark chocolate
50 g (2 oz) of unsalted butter
50 g (2 oz) of chopped walnuts (optional)
4 large eggs (separated)
Chocolate Squares (see opposite)

To prepare the mould:

Pour the cream into a 600 ml (1 pint) basin and whip to a soft consistency. Stir in 50 g (2 oz) of the grated chocolate and spread it to completely cover the inside of the basin. Transfer to a freezer bag and freeze for at least 24 hours.

For the filling:

Melt the remaining chocolate and butter together and allow to cool a little before stirring in the egg yolks and the walnuts. Whisk the egg whites to a stiff consistency and stir into the chocolate mixture. Pour into the frozen cream mould and refreeze for a minimum of 24 hours.

To serve:

Transfer from the freezer to the fridge and after an hour loosen it from the basin using a palette knife. Turn onto a serving dish and return it to the fridge until it has completely thawed (test by piercing the centre with a skewer). Spike with chocolate squares and serve.

Lazy Cook Tips

Allow several hours to completely thaw before serving, it will not collapse. This is a most useful pudding to keep in store. If you have bought too much cream, line a basin as described in the recipe and freeze – the centre filling can be added later. For ready-grated chocolate I use Charbonnel et Walker, Chocolat Charbonnel. For a very special occasion stick sparklers into the top and light to carry to the table. Remove before serving.

CHOCOLATE SQUARES

*Although it is now possible to buy small chocolate squares I
recommend you have a go at making these yourself.
They are much more delicate than any you can buy and it is so
satisfying to be able to say 'And I made the chocolate squares.'*

Spread approximately 50 g (2 oz) of dark melted chocolate onto a piece
of foil and allow to set before cutting into squares. Make in advance and
store in a box.

LAZY COOK TIPS

*They are so quick and easy to make and cost a fraction of the
price of the ones on sale.*

*An added advantage is that you can experiment with different
chocolate flavours – white, milk or dark*

*A disadvantage is that you might well end up eating the remaining
chocolate... So what, if it is a good quality chocolate it is good for
you – or so we are now told!*

Chocolate Blancmange

600 ml (1 pint) of whole milk
2 rounded dessertspoons of cornflour
1 rounded dessertspoon of cocoa powder (or drinking chocolate)
1 level tablespoon of granulated sugar

Mix the cornflour, cocoa powder and sugar to a smooth paste with a little of the milk.

Bring the remaining milk to a simmer, add the cornflour mixture and boil until it thickens, stirring continuously with a wooden spoon or spatula.

Taste for sweetness before pouring into a mould which has been dampened with cold water.

Leave in a fridge or cold larder to set.

To remove from the mould, loosen the sides using fingertips and shake the blancmange onto a serving plate.

Lazy Cook Tips

Animal-shaped moulds are fun to use when making chocolate blancmange for children.

If drinking chocolate is used, a little less sugar should be added.

CAKES & BISCUITS

Anyone who has ever volunteered to help at a charity fair or coffee morning will tell you that the stall they most enjoy manning is the cake stall. If truth be known, this is because everything is usually sold very quickly and they are then free to browse and hopefully buy, from the remaining stalls. Why is it that as a nation we love our cakes and biscuits so much? Could it be that we make them better than anyone else?

I hope you will find many tempting recipes here to make for home consumption or to put on a cake stall.

For very simple baking you can do with your kids, see also *Grandma, Can We Make Some Cakes?* (p263).

CAKES & BISCUITS

Moist Chocolate Cake

Ginger Cake

Birthday/Party Cheesecake

A Cake for a Crowd

Apple & Sultana Cake

Chocolate Vanilla Cake

Lemon & Fresh Strawberry Sandwich

Rock Cakes

Rich Walnut & Almond Cake

Almond Paste

Sacher Torte

Chocolate Icing

Sugar-Free Fruit Cake

Orange Bran Cake

Drop Scones

Scones (Fruit & Savoury)

Candied Peel Biscuits with Optional Orange Icing

Cheese Biscuits

Spicy Fruit Biscuits

Guidelines for Making Cakes & Biscuits

It will be noticed throughout this book that I use plain flour, and if a raising agent is needed, I add baking powder (1 teaspoon of baking powder to 100 g (4 oz) of plain flour).

When using a food processor, process the ingredients for a few seconds only. Food processors are as quick as magic and will cut down on the preparation time of many ingredients, which is my reason for constantly using one.

With few exceptions, always process dry ingredients first (flour, baking powder, sugar etc.), then add fat, eggs, milk and whatever liquid ingredients are included in the recipe. When a recipe includes dried fruits, or any ingredient which is not to be chopped finely, add these last and process for just a few seconds to mix them in, but not to chop. I recommend, as with most equipment, that the best quality food processor is purchased. I bought my food processor, the first on the market, over thirty years ago and it is still going strong.

If you do not have a food processor, for many of my recipes the ingredients can be blended using a hand-operated electric mixer, or the good old-fashioned wooden spoon.

When is it cooked?

Pastry and biscuits – when they begin to change colour and become crisp.

Sandwich or shallow cakes – when they rise in the tin and when lightly pressed in the centre, the mixture 'springs' back.

Deeper cakes (including fruit cakes) – when they begin to crack around the edge or in the centre. Test by piercing the centre with a metal skewer; if it comes out clean, the cake is cooked.

MOIST CHOCOLATE CAKE

Serves 8-10

175 g (6 oz) of unsalted butter (softened)
125 g (5 oz) of plain flour
2 teaspoons of baking powder
100 g (4 oz) of caster sugar
75 g (3 oz) of drinking chocolate
3 large eggs
1 teaspoon of vanilla essence
2 tablespoons of hot water
100 g (4 oz) of dark chocolate

Set the oven to gas mark 4/180°C/350°F/Aga baking oven.

Line the base of a 20 cm (8 inch) round cake tin with Bake-O-Glide, or lightly oiled greaseproof paper.

Put the flour, sugar, baking powder and drinking chocolate into a food processor and blend for a few seconds.

Add the butter, eggs, vanilla and boiling water and process again until smooth.

Pour the mixture into the prepared tin and bake for 35-45 minutes or until set.

Remove from oven and turn onto a wire tray.

Peel off the lining paper and grate chocolate over the surface of the cake while it is still hot.

Serve when cold or store in an airtight tin.

LAZY COOK TIPS

This makes a very moist chocolate cake. The grated chocolate will set as the cake cools leaving a chocolate topping.

To make it even richer, split the cake when it is cold and sandwich it together with redcurrant jelly.

GINGER CAKE

175 g (6 oz) of plain flour
1 heaped teaspoon of baking powder
75 g (3 oz) of soft cane sugar
½ teaspoon of ground ginger
50 g (2 oz) of margarine (softened)
50 g (2 oz) of lard (softened)
1 teaspoon of fresh lemon juice
3 large eggs
50 g (2 oz) of ginger preserved in syrup (cut up)
1 tablespoon of ginger syrup

Set the oven to gas mark 4/180°C/350°F/Aga baking oven.

Line the sides and base of a 450 g (1 lb) loaf tin with a strip of oiled foil or greaseproof paper.

Blend all the dry ingredients in a food processor for a few seconds. Add all remaining ingredients and process until smooth.

Pour into the prepared tin and bake in the preheated oven for 30-40 minutes or until set.

Turn onto a wire tray to cool. Store in an airtight tin.

LAZY COOK TIPS

Give this added interest by spreading the top of the cooked cake with lemon curd or honey. Sprinkle over a mixture of chopped crystallised ginger, glacé cherries and walnuts and press down to secure.

BIRTHDAY/PARTY CHEESECAKE

An alternative to a fruit cake.

Serves 8 – 12

SELECTION OF CHEESE:
50 g (2 oz) of Shropshire blue (grated)
50 g (2 oz) of Mull of Kintyre (grated)
100 g (4 oz) of farmhouse Lancashire (grated)
100 g (4 oz) of Strathdon Blue (grated)
75 g (3 oz) of May Hill Green
150 g (6 oz) packet of peppered Boursin
100 g (4 oz) of curd or cream cheese

TO GARNISH:
Small handful of dried bay leaves
Walnut halves
Finely grated parsley
Cream cheese for sticking

Mix all the cheeses together and shape into a 15 cm (6 inch) cake.

Cover and leave in a fridge until firm.

Place on a cake board and stick (using cream cheese) small dried bay leaves and walnut halves around the sides.

Top with more walnuts, bay leaves and finely grated parsley.

Serve, with ceremony, as a cheese course.

LAZY COOK TIPS

I made this for my son Will's 40th birthday family celebration lunch and it was a great success. On the top I arranged finely chopped parsley in the shape of '40'.

I used the above cheeses but as long as there is a mixture of firm and soft cheeses to hold it together, make your own choice. It is rich and filling – serve in small slices.

A CAKE FOR A CROWD

A wartime recipe.

1 x 500 g (1 lb) bag of self-raising flour
2 level teaspoons of mixed spice
1 level teaspoon of baking powder
225 g (8 oz) of caster sugar
1 x 250 g block of margarine (cut into small pieces)
1 x 500 g (1 lb) bag of mixed dried fruit
5 large eggs (whisked together)
Approximately 5 tablespoons of milk

GLAZE:
1 tablespoon of milk
2 tablespoons of granulated sugar

Set the oven to gas mark 4/180°C/350°F/Aga baking oven.

Line a 30 cm (12 inch) square cake tin (or a similar sized meat tin) with greased foil.

Process the flour, caster sugar, spice, baking powder and margarine to a breadcrumb consistency, then transfer to a large mixing bowl.

Stir in the dried fruit. Add the eggs and milk and, using a wooden spoon, mix all together to a sticky consistency (add more milk if necessary).

Spread into the prepared tin and smooth the top, brush with milk and scatter with granulated sugar.

Bake in the preheated oven for 45-60 minutes or until baked – test by piercing a metal skewer into the centre and continue cooking if necessary. Remove from the tin and cool on a wire tray. Cut into wedges to serve.

LAZY COOK TIPS

I cannot take credit for this recipe which was given to me by my sister Elsie, who in turn was handed it down from her late mother-in-law. It is a cake to make for a crowd or for a fund-raising event, or to make and freeze in wedges to serve to unexpected teatime guests.

APPLE & SULTANA CAKE

Moist and good.

225 g (8 oz) of plain flour
2 teaspoons of baking powder
100 g (4 oz) of demerara (or soft brown) sugar
150 g (5 oz) of margarine (softened)
2 large eggs
4 tablespoons of milk
1 large Bramley cooking apple (peeled, cored and roughly chopped)
225 g (8 oz) of sultanas
1 teaspoon of cinnamon powder
A little extra demerara sugar for topping

Set the oven to gas mark 4/180°C/350°F/Aga baking oven.

Drop a parchment cake liner into an 18 cm (7 inch) round cake tin with a loose base.

Process the flour, sugar and baking powder together for a few seconds. Add the margarine, eggs and milk and process until smooth.

Add the chopped apple and the sultanas and process for a few seconds to mix in.

Pack the mixture into the lined tin and scatter the top with cinnamon powder and about a tablespoon of demerara sugar.

Stand the tin on a baking tray and bake in the preheated oven for 1-1½ hours or until set (test with a skewer). Remove from oven and allow to cool for a few minutes before removing from the tin onto a wire tray. When cold, store in an airtight tin.

LAZY COOK TIPS

This makes a deliciously moist cake. Use Bramley apples if available – chop them roughly and not too small; finding apple chunks in the baked cake adds to the enjoyment.

You may need to add a little more milk to create a smooth mixture. The cinnamon gives a good, spicy flavour and the sugar topping adds sparkle.

Chocolate Vanilla Cake

This is a light and delicious cake without being too sweet.

100 g (4 oz) of plain flour
1 heaped teaspoon of baking powder
50 g (2 oz) of caster sugar
100 g (4 oz) of unsalted butter (softened)
3 large eggs
½ teaspoon of vanilla extract
50 g (2 oz) of grated dark chocolate

Set the oven to gas mark 4/180°C/350°F/Aga baking oven.

Drop a parchment cake liner into a 15 cm (6 inch) round cake tin with a loose base.

Blend the flour, baking powder and sugar in a food processor for a few seconds.

Add the butter, eggs and vanilla and continue to process until smooth.

Spread half the mixture into the lined tin, cover with half the grated chocolate, then top with the remaining cake mixture.

Smooth the top before covering with the remaining grated chocolate.

Stand the tin on a baking tray and bake in the preheated oven for approximately 40 minutes or until set (test with a skewer).

Lazy Cook Tips

I recommend keeping a tin of Charbonnel et Walker, Chocolat Charbonnel in your store cupboard. It may seem extravagant but it is a good quality chocolate, will save time on grating and will prevent you eating the remainder of a chocolate bar!

Store in an airtight tin and eat within 4 days.

Lemon & Fresh Strawberry Sandwich

Serves 8
100 g (4 oz) of plain flour
1 teaspoon of baking powder
75 g (3 oz) of caster sugar
100 g (4 oz) of margarine (softened)
2 large eggs
2 lemons
1 jar (411 g) of lemon curd
225 g (8 oz) of fresh strawberries
100 g (4 oz) of icing sugar

Set the oven to gas mark 4/180°C/350°F/Aga baking oven.

Grease or oil two 18 cm (7 inch) sandwich tins.

Mix the flour, sugar and baking powder in a food processor for a few seconds. Add the margarine and eggs and process until smooth.

Spread the mixture between the prepared tins and bake for 20 minutes or until set – remove from the tins and place onto a wire tray to cool.

To assemble, remove and keep the zest from one lemon and squeeze the juice over each cake, then spread with lemon curd and sandwich together with strawberry halves, or slices.

Mix the icing sugar to a spreadable consistency with lemon juice and spread over the top of the sandwich.

Mark into 8 slices, put a whole strawberry on each slice and scatter the reserved lemon zest in the centre.

Lazy Cook Tips

The icing should not be too stiff. Pour it onto the top sandwich; if some runs down the side, it does not matter. Always remove the zest from fruits before squeezing. The cooked cakes can be frozen and assembled and decorated when required. A delicious cake to serve in the summer for tea or as a pudding.

ROCK CAKES

*I have always loved the slightly dry texture and
spicy flavour of these little cakes*

Makes 10-12
225 g (8 oz) of plain flour
2 teaspoons of baking powder
75 g (3 oz) of demerara sugar
½ teaspoon of mixed spice
50 g (2 oz) of margarine
25 g (1 oz) of lard
1 large egg
1 tablespoon of milk
100 g (4 oz) of currants or sultanas
A little runny honey (optional)

QUICK
FIX

Set the oven to gas mark 4/180°C/350°F/Aga baking oven.

Lightly grease or oil a baking tray.

Put the flour and baking powder into a large bowl, add the fats (cut into small pieces) and rub in until you achieve a breadcrumb texture.

Add the remaining ingredients (except the honey) and mix to a sticky paste.

Using two forks, pile into rocky heaps onto the prepared baking tray and bake for 10-15 minutes or until brown and crisp.

Put on a wire tray and pour a little runny honey onto each hot cake (optional).

Allow to cool before eating.

LAZY COOK TIPS

These are best eaten the day they are made — not usually a problem!

Rich Walnut & Almond Cake

225 g (8 oz) of unsalted butter (softened)
100 g (4 oz) of plain flour
1 teaspoon of baking powder
50 g (2 oz) of ground almonds
175 g (6 oz) of soft brown sugar
4 large eggs
1 tablespoon of sweet sherry
100 g (4 oz) of walnut pieces

Set the oven to gas mark 4/180°C/350°F/Aga baking oven.

Mix the flour, baking powder, ground almonds and sugar in a food processor for a few seconds.

Add the butter, eggs and sherry and mix until smooth.

Mix in the walnuts and process for a few seconds only.

Pour the resulting mixture into the lined tin, smooth the top, stand the tin on a baking tray and bake in the preheated oven for 45 minutes to 1 hour or until set (test with a metal skewer).

Remove it from the oven and after a few minutes remove from the tin onto a wire tray.

When cold, store in an airtight tin or polythene bag, or freeze.

Lazy Cook Tips

This is a good cake to bake in the autumn when the new season's walnuts are available.

It also makes an excellent alternative to a traditional rich Christmas cake, when I would suggest the top is lightly spread with apricot jam or lemon curd, then covered with almond paste (see opposite) and decorated with whole almonds and walnut halves.

Almond Paste

To cover a 25.5 cm (10 inch) round cake:
350 g (12 oz) of ground almonds
275 g (10 oz) of caster sugar
275 g (10 oz) of icing sugar
2 tablespoons of brandy
2 tablespoons of fresh lemon juice
1 teaspoon of orange flower water
A few spots of almond essence
1 teaspoon of vanilla essence
1 medium-sized egg
1 egg yolk

Mix the almonds and sugars together in a large bowl and make a well in the centre.

Whisk all remaining ingredients together, pour into the well and work together to form a paste.

Shape, or roll on a surface sifted with icing sugar.

Lazy Cook Tips

Try not to overknead this paste; it will extract the oil from the almonds and will eventually cause a top icing to discolour.

Use as soon as it is made, otherwise it will become crisp on the surface and difficult to handle.

If it is too sticky, add a little more sifted icing sugar. If too dry, add a little more brandy or lemon juice.

SACHER TORTE

A superb Viennese cake which can also be served as a pudding.

100 g (4 oz) of unsalted butter (softened)
75 g (3 oz) of caster sugar
4 large eggs (separated)
175 g (6 oz) of dark chocolate (melted)
100 g (4 oz) of ground almonds
1 teaspoon of instant coffee granules (stir into 1 tablespoon of hot water
Chocolate icing (optional, see opposite)

Set the oven to gas mark 4/180°C/350°F/Aga baking oven.

Drop a parchment cake liner into a 15-18 cm (6-7 inch) cake tin.

Using an electric hand mixer, combine the butter, sugar and egg yolks in a large bowl until they are light and fluffy.

Stir in the melted chocolate, ground almonds and coffee. In a separate bowl, whisk the egg whites until they are stiff and stir these into the chocolate mixture.

Pour the mixture into the prepared tin, and stand this on a baking tray and bake in the preheated oven for approximately 45 minutes to 1 hour (test with a metal skewer).

Cool a little before removing it from the tin onto a wire tray. When cold, store in a covered container in a fridge, or freeze.

Serve small slices. For extra richness, top it with chocolate icing.

This cake is also an excellent standby to serve as a pudding and especially useful if entertaining over a few days.

Turn each slice on its side and top with a generous spoonful of whipped double cream and a chocolate truffle.

LAZY COOK TIPS

I would recommend it is cut into slices to freeze. This is an excellent cake to serve to those who are unable to eat flour or wheat.

CHOCOLATE ICING

*The flavour of this particular chocolate icing recipe provides
a perfect topping for a chocolate torte or similar
rich chocolate cakes.*

100 g (4 oz) of dark chocolate
25 g (1 oz) of unsalted butter
1 teaspoon of instant coffee granules

Melt the chocolate and butter together in a microwave, in a basin over a pan of hot water, or on the surface of an Aga.

Dissolve the coffee granules in a tablespoon of warm water — stir all ingredients together and pour over the cake.

SUGAR-FREE FRUIT CAKE

If you are trying to diet but crave a slice of cake, this is the recipe for you.

225 g (8 oz) of plain flour
2 teaspoons of baking powder
1 teaspoon of mixed spice
100 g (4 oz) of margarine (softened)
2 large eggs
100 ml (4 fl oz) of milk
½ teaspoon of vanilla extract
225 g (8 oz) of mixed dried fruit
6-8 walnut halves (optional)

Set the oven to gas mark 4/180°C/350°F/Aga baking oven.

Drop a parchment cake liner into an 18 cm (7 inch) cake tin.

Mix the flour, baking powder and spice in a food processor, add the margarine, eggs, milk and vanilla extract and blend until smooth.

Add the dried fruit, processing only for a few moments.

Pour the mixture into the prepared tin, smooth the top and press walnut halves round the edge.

Stand the tin on a baking tray and bake for 1¼-1½ hours, or until set (test with a metal skewer).

Remove the cake from the oven and after a few minutes remove the cake from the tin, leaving it to cool on a wire tray. Slice to serve.

Store in an airtight tin or container.

LAZY COOK TIPS

This cake is popular with anyone following a sugar-free diet.

But remember that although no sugar is added to this recipe, mixed dried fruit does contain a little sugar.

Check before serving to someone with diabetes.

Orange Bran Cake

175 g (6 oz) of softened butter or margarine
150 g (5 oz) plain flour
2 teaspoons of baking powder
25 g (1 oz) of bran
125 g (5 oz) of soft brown sugar
3 large eggs
4 tablespoons of freshly squeezed orange juice

Optional topping
100 g (4 oz) of icing sugar
1 orange (zest and juice)

The Cake

Set the oven at gas mark 4/ 180°C/ 360°F/Aga baking oven.

Place a cake liner into a 15-18 cm (6-7 inch) round cake tin.

Blend the flour, baking powder, bran and sugar in a processor for a few seconds. Add the remaining ingredients and process until smooth.

Pour the mixture into the lined tin, stand it on a baking tray and bake in the preset oven for 30-45 minutes or until set (test with a metal skewer).

Remove from the oven and leave to stand for a few minutes, then take out of the tin and cool on a wire tray.

The Icing

Mix the icing sugar and orange juice to a smooth paste, spread over the cold cake and scatter with orange zest. Serve when the icing has set. Store in an airtight tin and serve within 3 days.

Lazy Cook Tips

Concentrated orange juice can be used in the cake, but freshly squeezed is best.

Remove the zest from oranges before squeezing.

Drop Scones

The children in my family loved these and we all remember the occasion when our eldest son Edward took over the cooking and shaped them to form the words 'Happy Christmas!'

QUICK
FIX

Makes 12-20
225 g (8 oz) of plain flour
½ teaspoon of bicarbonate of soda
1 teaspoon of cream of tartar
1 teaspoon of caster sugar
1 large egg
200 ml (8 fl oz) of milk

Blend all the ingredients in a processor until smooth.

Heat a heavy-based frying pan and rub the base with a little lard or oil.

With the mixture, make circular-shaped 'rounds' in the pan using a dessertspoon.

When the surface rises and bubbles, turn them over using a large metal spatula or fish slice.

Cook until the reverse side is slightly browned, then remove from pan and keep warm in a clean tea cloth until all of the mixture is used.

Serve, or freeze when cold.

The scones can be served warm or cold and should be spread with softened butter.

Work a little cinnamon or mixed spice into the butter to add a different flavour.

For savoury presentation, spread them with a little cream cheese or pâté and top with salad ingredients or a curl of Parma ham, chicken, meat, fish — the choice is yours.

LAZY COOK TIPS

Omit the sugar if serving these with savoury ingredients.

The pan should be moderately hot before the mixture is added and it should only be necessary to grease it at the beginning of cooking.

Aga users should raise the simmering plate lid for a few minutes to allow it to cool slightly before cooking commences.

Vary the size of the scones by dropping the mixture from a table-, dessert- or teaspoon, dropping it from the tip of the spoon to form 'rounds', or from the side for an oval shape. An alternative method of mixing is to put all the dry ingredients in a large bowl or basin and make a well in the centre.

Whisk the egg lightly, stir in the milk and pour this, a little at a time, into the flour well, mixing with a wooden spoon until the mixture turns to a smooth paste.

Scones

I was taught that scones should be 'quick to make and quick to bake'.

Makes approximately 12
225 g (8 oz) of plain white flour (or ½ white and ½ wholemeal flours)
2 heaped teaspoons of baking powder
1 teaspoon of sugar (caster or granulated)
50 g (2 oz) of unsalted butter
1 egg whisked and made up to 150 ml (5 fl oz) with milk

Set the oven to gas mark 7/220°C /425°F/Aga roasting oven.

Blitz the flour, baking powder and sugar in a food processor for a few seconds.

Add the butter (cut into small pieces), processing again for a few seconds before pouring in the milk mixture until a ball of dough is formed.

Remove from the processor onto a lightly floured surface.

With floured hands, mould it into a round shape, pressing down until it is approximately 3 cm (1inch) thick.

Cut this into smaller round shapes using a 4 cm (1½ inch) fluted or plain cutter and place on a lightly oiled baking tray.

Brush the tops with milk or beaten egg and bake for 5-10 minutes, or until well risen and brown on top.

Remove from oven and cool on a wire tray.

Lazy Cook Tips

Sour cream or buttermilk can be used in place of fresh milk.

A little extra liquid may be needed when making wholemeal scones. Eat scones the day they are baked.

They can be quickly mixed by hand by stirring the flour, baking powder and sugar in a large mixing bowl, then rubbing in the butter pieces and stirring in the milk mixture until a dough is formed (follow instructions for shaping and baking as above).

CHERRY OR FRUIT SCONES:

Add 50 g (2 oz) of glacé cherries or mixed dried fruit to the plain scone recipe.

SAVOURY SCONES

CHEESE:

Omit the sugar, reduce the flour to 175 g (6 oz) and add 50 g (2 oz) of strongly flavoured grated cheese.

Serve hot, split and spread with butter.

Alternatively, omit the butter and spread with a spoon of chutney, tomato, or olive pesto.

Garnish with a scattering of mustard cress.

HERB:

Leave out the sugar and add 2 tablespoons of freshly chopped mixed herbs.

If mixing in a food processor, the herbs should be processed before the other ingredients are added.

Serve warm or hot. Split and spread with butter (optional) and fish, meat or pâté.

These can be sandwiched together or left open. Garnish with a few leaves of mustard cress.

CANDIED PEEL BISCUITS WITH OPTIONAL ORANGE ICING

Makes 20-25
150 g (5 oz) of plain flour
25 g (1 oz) of caster sugar
100 g (4 oz) of margarine (cut into small pieces)
100 g (4 oz) of mixed candied peel (chopped)
1 tablespoon of orange juice (fresh or from a carton)
Orange icing (optional)

Set oven to gas mark 4/180°C/350°F/Aga baking oven.

Lightly grease a large baking tray. Process the flour and sugar for a few seconds, add the remaining ingredients and process until a ball of paste is formed.

Spoon generous teaspoons of the mixture onto the prepared baking tray. Flatten with a wet fork and bake for 15-20 minutes or until a golden biscuit colour. Remove from oven and cool on a wire tray.

When cool, spread the base of each biscuit with orange icing (recipe below). Store in an airtight container.

LAZY COOK TIPS

If a fresh orange is used the zest also can be added to the mixture to give a more intense flavour. The biscuits can be served with or without the additional icing, but I feel sure you will prefer them with!

ORANGE ICING

100 g (4 oz) of icing sugar
2 tablespoons of orange juice

Sieve the icing sugar into a bowl and mix in 2 tablespoons of orange juice. Stir together to form a spreadable icing.

CHEESE BISCUITS

Makes 20-25
100 g (4 oz) of plain flour
2 generous pinches of cayenne pepper
2 generous pinches of mustard powder
50 g (2 oz) of margarine (cut into small pieces)
75 g (3 oz) of strong Cheddar (cut into small pieces)
A few dashes of Worcestershire sauce
2 tablespoons of cold water

Set oven to gas mark 4/180°C/350°F/Aga baking oven. Lightly grease a baking tray.

Put all the ingredients (except the water) into a food processor and process for a few seconds into a breadcrumb consistency.

Adding the water, process until a paste is formed.

Put onto a lightly floured board or surface, or directly onto the prepared baking tray and roll out thinly.

Cut into squares and bake for 15-20 minutes or until the biscuits are golden and crisp.

Cool on a wire rack. Store in an airtight container.

LAZY COOK TIPS

Following my preferred method of rolling directly onto the baking tray, it is essential to grease rather than oil the baking tray to prevent the paste moving whilst rolling.

Should the outer biscuits colour before the centre is cooked, remove them and continue to cook the remaining biscuits until crisp.

The outer uneven shapes can be served; they indicate that they are proudly 'home-made'.

SPICY FRUIT BISCUITS

Makes 35-40
175 g (6 oz) of margarine (softened)
225 g (8 oz) of plain white flour
75 g (3 oz) of demerara sugar
1 teaspoon of mixed spice
100 g (4 oz) of raisins
2 tablespoons of milk

Set oven to gas mark 4/180°C/350°F/Aga baking oven.

Lightly oil a baking tray.

Process the flour, sugar and spice for a few seconds. Add the margarine, raisins and milk and process to a paste.

Put generous teaspoons of the mixture onto the prepared baking tray and flatten with a wet fork.

Bake in the preheated oven for 20-30 minutes or until they begin to turn a golden biscuit colour.

Cool on a wire tray and, when cold, store in an airtight tin.

LAZY COOK TIPS

The speed of mixing the ingredients in a food processor and shaping the biscuits using my Lazy Cook method makes biscuit making so simple.

This will help to reduce your supermarket bill by pounds.

FOOD FOR HUNGRY LITTLE TUMS

New mums often find themselves cooking separate meals for their babies but this really isn't necessary. No matter at what stage of weaning your child is, whether they are eating just fruit and vegetables or have moved on to meat, fish and pasta and potatoes, my Lazy Cook recipes provide a wholesome meal.

Make enough for the whole family and portion, purée or freeze some for baby, building up a selection of 'ready meals' for a later date (keep them in a freezer for no longer than two months before serving).

Introduce your little ones to new flavours gradually. Present their food in small portions and they will often eat more than if they were given one single large amount.

Children are attracted by shapes and colours. Introduce these as often as you can, perhaps in the form of a garnish on tea-time sandwiches which can be decorated with small pieces of raw carrot, salad or fruit.

Remember that you are setting their eating patterns for life and the more quickly and easily they accept good wholesome food, the more healthy they will become in adult life. My children started the day with a teaspoon of cod liver oil and ended it with a mug of milky cocoa. This is doubtless considered old fashioned now, but they grew up strong and healthy and rarely missed school through illness.

FOOD FOR HUNGRY LITTLE TUMS

Tomato & Lentil Soup

Annie's Cheese Pie

Chicken Casserole

Quick Cheesy, Herby Vegetables

Baked Bean Pie

Fish in Batter served with Tomato Sauce

Fish Fingers

Marrow & Tomato Bake

Puffed-Up Chicken with a Tapenade Sauce

TOMATO & LENTIL SOUP

Serves 6-8

2 large onions (skinned and roughly chopped)
800 g tin of chopped tomatoes in natural juices
410 g tin of lentils in water
1 large orange (juice and zest)
1 teaspoon of runny honey
¼ teaspoon of mixed dried herbs
900 ml (1½ pints) of vegetable stock
Freshly ground black pepper

QUICK
FIX

Boil a little water in a large pan, add the prepared onion, cover and cook until softened. Add the tomatoes and, using an electric hand whisk, purée the ingredients whilst in the pan.

Add all the remaining ingredients, stir and simmer for 10 minutes before serving.

LAZY COOK TIPS

The vibrant colour of this soup will appeal to children.

Add chunks of wholemeal bread for extra nourishment and to make it easier for 'learners' to eat.

ANNIE'S CHEESE PIE

*I have adapted this recipe from a similar pie we as a family were
served many years ago when we visited our friend Annie.
I baked it many times when the children were at home and it has become a
family favourite, affectionately known as ACP (Annie's Cheese Pie).*

Serves 6-8
225 g (8 oz) of plain white (or wholemeal) flour
100 g (4 oz) of lard
50-75 ml (2-3 fl oz) of cold water
1 large onion (skinned and chopped)
1 tablespoon of olive oil
1 x 227 g tin of chopped tomatoes
A pinch of sugar
A good sprinkling of herbs (fresh or dried)
175 g (6 oz) of strong cheese (grated)
150 ml (¼ pint) of warmed milk
3 large eggs
Freshly ground white pepper
Several pinches of English mustard powder

Set the oven to gas mark 6/200°C/400°F/Aga roasting oven.

TO MAKE THE PASTRY:

Blend the flour and fat in a food processor for a few seconds, then slowly
add the water until a ball of pastry begins to form.

Lightly oil a deep pie dish and roll out the pastry large enough to line the
base and sides. Prick the base with a fork and bake in the preheated oven
for 15-20 minutes.

Remove from the oven and reduce the temperature (gas mark 4/
180°C/350°F/Aga baking oven).

TO MAKE THE PIE:

Heat the oil in a pan, add the prepared onion and cook until it begins to soften.

Remove from the pan and spread the onion over the base of the cooked pastry.

Top with tomatoes seasoned with sugar and herbs, and then with grated cheese.

In a separate bowl, whisk the eggs, then combine with the warmed milk, the pepper and mustard powder.

Pour the mixture through a sieve onto the cheese and bake for around 1 hour, or until it has set and is brown on top.

Serve straight from the oven with boiled rice.

LAZY COOK TIPS

This is an excellent pie and so quick to prepare. It does not matter how unevenly the pastry is rolled or patched when lining the dish and there is no need to use baking beans to prevent the pastry base from rising — it doesn't matter if it does!

It's a good recipe for using up any odd ends of cheese.

CHICKEN CASSEROLE

Serves 8

2 large onions (skinned and sliced)

4 chicken legs (dried on kitchen roll)

6 rindless rashers of bacon (each cut into 3 pieces)

450 g (1 lb) of mushrooms (wiped with damp kitchen roll)

1 tablespoon of mushroom ketchup

1 teaspoon of dried tarragon

800 g tin of chopped tomatoes in natural juices

1 teaspoon of runny honey

300 ml (10 fl oz) of stock or water

340 g tin of sweetcorn in natural juices

Set oven at gas mark 6/200°C/400°F/Aga roasting oven.

Heat a little water in a large casserole or pan with a lid, add the onion, cover and cook for a few minutes until beginning to soften.

Remove and discard the skin from each chicken leg. Separate the chicken thighs from the drumsticks, then add to the pan with all the remaining ingredients, except the sweetcorn.

Cover and put into the preheated oven until it begins to simmer. Reduce the oven temperature to gas mark 3/160°C/325°F/Aga simmering oven and continue to cook for one hour. Stir in the sweetcorn and juices towards the end of cooking.

Serve hot from the oven or, when cold, store in a fridge and heat to serve a day or two later. Use within 4 days.

LAZY COOK TIPS

Chicken legs are usually a good buy and because they are cooked on the bone the flavour is improved. If, like me, you simply cannot throw anything away, the chicken skins can be simmered in water to make a stock. Pour some water in the empty tomato tin and then add this to the casserole. I use white mushrooms in this particular casserole; cut them into halves or quarters if they are large.

QUICK CHEESY, HERBY VEGETABLES

Quick Fix

Serves 6

1 medium-sized cauliflower (broken into small florets)
1 head of calabrese - similar size to cauliflower (broken into small florets)
12 small carrots (scrubbed, topped and tailed)
50 g (2 oz) of Double Gloucester cheese
50 g (2 oz) of Stilton cheese
Mixed herbs: marjoram, oregano, sage, mint, parsley, lemon balm (roughly chopped)

Wash all the vegetables under a cold running tap.

Boil approximately 600 ml (1 pint) of water in a large saucepan.

Add the carrots, put the lid on the pan and boil until they begin to soften.

Add the cauliflower and calabrese (add a little more boiling water if necessary).

While the vegetables are cooking, grate the cheeses and chop the herbs.

When all the vegetables have cooked to your liking, remove the pan from heat.

Drain off all but 2-3 tablespoons of cooking water, then immediately stir in the cheeses and herbs. Serve hot.

LAZY COOK TIPS

As the cheese melts, the water left in the pan will turn into a delicious liquid.

This is a most colourful way of serving a selection of vegetables as well as being very tasty.

BAKED BEAN PIE

This is a 'must' for busy weekends or children's parties.

Serves — any number!
1 leek or large onion (sliced)
Mushrooms (chopped or sliced)
Cooked sausages (sliced)
Leftover pieces of cooked bacon, ham or chicken
1 large tin of baked beans
100 ml (4 fl oz) of milk
Garlic (optional)
Freshly ground black pepper
1 teaspoon of mushroom ketchup
Worcestershire sauce (several good dashes)
A few pinches of dried herbs
1 teaspoon of tomato purée
Mashed potato (see opposite)
Grated cheese

Top and tail the leek and cut into roughly 1 cm (½ inch) rings (including the dark-green stem). Wash thoroughly in a colander under a cold running water tap.

Boil a small amount of water in a large pan, then add the leeks. Cover and boil until they begin to soften (about 2 minutes).

Strain off any excess liquid and stir in the remaining ingredients (except the mashed potato and cheese).

Put into an ovenproof dish, cover with mashed potato and sprinkle over the grated cheese.

Heat under a grill, or in a hot oven (gas mark 6/200°C/400°F/ Aga roasting oven) until crisp and brown on top.

Serve with warm bread.

MASHED POTATO

Peel and cut the potatoes into small pieces before boiling them until soft.

Strain off the liquid, add a little milk, a generous helping of butter and several gratings of nutmeg and mash together until smooth.

LAZY COOK TIPS

The quantities in this recipe vary depending on the numbers of people being served and the amounts of leftover ingredients available – i.e. a 'fridge tidy' meal!

The mashed potato can be prepared using either packeted or fresh potatoes.

The cheese topping is optional – if it is not used, you can brush the potato with beaten egg or melted butter instead.

I find the best way to cover the pie ingredients with mashed potato is by adding it in small amounts using a knife and beginning at the edge of the dish then filling towards the centre.

It is one of those tasks which is rarely demonstrated and not always easily achieved.

FISH IN BATTER SERVED WITH TOMATO SAUCE

This serves 2-3 as starters, or make a larger quantity and pile them onto a dish for people to help themselves. Children will love this dish; it's an excellent way to introduce them to 'real' fish.

Makes approximately 12
150 ml (5 fl oz) of batter mixture
225 g (8 oz) of cooked prawns
A little olive oil

Make the batter in advance (see recipe opposite).

Set the oven to gas mark 6/200°C/400°F/Aga roasting oven.

Using a 12-hole patty tin, pour a teaspoon of oil into each hole and put in the preheated oven for 1-2 minutes, or until hot.

Whisk a tablespoon of cold water into the batter mixture and pour it into the hot oil (½ to ¾ full) and drop a few prawns into each.

Return to the oven and bake for 10-15 minutes or until well risen and golden. Serve hot from the oven with the tomato sauce (recipe opposite).

LAZY COOK TIPS

These are really quick to make and bake – they are light in texture and quite delicious.

The fillings can be varied i.e. a mixture of shellfish, cod, salmon, haddock etc.

Batter Mixture

100 g (4 oz) of plain flour
300 ml (10 fl oz) of milk
2 large eggs
1 tablespoon of olive oil

Blend the flour, milk, eggs and oil in a food processor or liquidiser until smooth.

Cover the mixture and put in a fridge or cold larder for a minimum of 30 minutes to allow the batter to thicken.

Before cooking, whisk in a tablespoon of cold water. Follow individual recipes for oven temperatures and cooking times.

Lazy Cook Tips

The recommended 'resting' time allows the starch grains in the flour to swell and thicken the batter. The addition of cold water will release steam during cooking which will lighten the batter.

Tomato Sauce

Tomato ketchup
Fresh lemon juice
Sun-dried tomato paste
Runny honey

For each tablespoon of tomato ketchup, add one teaspoon of lemon juice and one teaspoon of sun-dried tomato paste. Stir over a gentle heat until hot. If too sharp, sweeten with a little runny honey. Serve hot or cold. Increase quantities to make a larger amount.

FISH FINGERS

An ideal recipe to introduce children to fresh fish.

QUICK
FIX

White fish fillets (dried on kitchen roll)
Breadcrumbs (fresh or dried – see p223)
A little olive oil

Set the oven to gas mark 6/200°C/400°F/Aga roasting oven.

Remove any bones and cut the fillets into strips.

Place them in a lightly oiled, shallow ovenproof dish and sprinkle with fresh or dried breadcrumbs and top with a dash of oil.

Bake for 6-8 minutes or until the strips of fish are firm to the touch and the breadcrumbs are turning golden.

Allow to cool for a few minutes before serving as individual fingers to children.

LAZY COOK TIPS

When my children were young this was my home-made version of fish fingers.

Make sure all bones are removed before cooking the fish; even fish bought as 'fillets' often contains a bone or two.

MARROW & TOMATO BAKE

Serves 6-8
1 marrow
A handful of fresh sage leaves
400 g tin of chopped tomatoes in natural juices
A pinch of granulated sugar
Freshly ground white pepper
100 g (4 oz) of grated cheese (a mixture of Stilton and Cheddar)

Set oven to gas mark 6/200°C/400°F/Aga roasting oven.

Wash and top and tail the marrow. Cut it in half lengthways and discard the centre seeds.

Slice each half marrow into three lengths and cut each of these into slices approximately 5 mm (¼ inch) thick.

Cook in a little boiling water for about a minute to begin the softening process.

Using a slotted spoon, transfer them to a large, shallow ovenproof dish and scatter with the sage.

Cover with the tinned tomatoes and juice. Add a good pinch of sugar and season with freshly ground pepper.

Top with the grated cheese and bake, uncovered, in the preheated oven for 20-30 minutes or until hot.

Serve hot with a summer roast.

LAZY COOK TIPS

This has become one of the most favourite summer vegetables I serve. It can be prepared in advance and stored, covered, in a fridge or cold larder in readiness for putting into the oven.

It is a good way of using up all the bits of cheese in the fridge, and for an alternative topping, mix them with some dried breadcrumbs (brown or white).

Puffed-Up Chicken with a Tapenade Sauce

Serves 4

4 skinless chicken breasts

1 sheet of frozen uncooked ready-rolled puff pastry

(approximately 280 x 215 cm each)

1 jar of tapenade (green olive paste)

Set oven at gas mark 7/220°C /425°F//Aga roasting oven.

Lightly oil a baking tray or tin. Cut the defrosted sheet of pastry into 4 pieces and spread a teaspoon of tapenade paste down the centre of each.

Top with a chicken breast and enclose it in the pastry (like a sausage roll). Dampen the edges to seal together.

Place onto the prepared tray, sealed pastry ends down.

Prick across the top with a fork and bake in the preheated oven for 10-15 minutes or until the pastry has risen and browned slightly.

Serve immediately with my Tapenade Sauce (see opposite).

Lazy Cook tips

The pastry helps to keep the breasts moist. Test that they are cooked by piercing the centre of the pastry towards the base.

Children will enjoy the Puffed-Up Chicken, although they may prefer a tomato sauce or ketchup in place of the tapenade.

TAPENADE SAUCE

*On arrival at a venue to give a talk, I was touched when
a member of the audience came up to me and told me how much
they enjoyed this chicken dish and accompanying tapenade sauce.
She said that everyone she served it to loved this meal and that
she was so impressed by how quick and easy it was to make.*

50 ml (2 fl oz) of white wine
50 ml (2 fl oz) of vegetable or chicken stock
2 teaspoons of tapenade or green olive paste
Fresh fennel fern (if available)
2 teaspoons of double cream

Put the wine and stock into a pan and boil to reduce by half.
Stir in the remaining ingredients and serve.

LAZY COOK TIPS

If making this sauce to serve with fish, use fish stock.

Cut the feathery strands off the fennel stalk and discard the stalk.

*This sauce can be stored when cold, covered, in a fridge or cold
larder. Use within 3 days.*

*Tapenade or green olive paste is available from supermarkets or
delicatessens.*

Lazy Cook Notes

GRANDMA, CAN WE MAKE SOME CAKES?

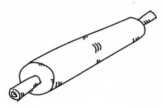

Charlie, our grandson is a little too young as yet to help in the kitchen but I know from my sisters and friends how their grandchildren love learning how to cook, and especially helping to make cakes and biscuits.

It is often something their mother's have little time to do, but when visiting Grandma, time passes quickly when little fingers set to work on the flour and fat! Their concentration is a joy to behold even though the tasting is often something else!

Because these recipes are intended to be made with the help of children, I have in some cases recommended a more traditional method of mixing the ingredients by hand but as you can see from the Lazy Cook tips, they can be mixed more quickly by an older child or an adult using a food processor.

Always remember to ask parents if the children have any special dietary requirements, allergies, immunities etc.

When toddlers and children are in the kitchen, keep knives and sharp and hot implements well out of reach of little fingers.

Always turn saucepan handles towards the centre of the hob – I find this a good practice at all times.

In addition to the recipes included in this section, please look through the main index where I feel sure you will find many more recipes suitable for cooking with the help of your grandchildren. What better way could there be of family bonding?

GRANDMA, CAN WE MAKE SOME CAKES?

Muffins from Mars

Gingerbread Biscuits & Shapes

Honey Oat Biscuits

Cranberry & Chocolate Rocks

Date & Oat Chocolate Blocks

Chocolate Wholemeal Biscuits

Picnic Slices

Muffins from Mars

Little cakes with a surprise filling.

Makes 8
100 g (4 oz) of plain flour
1 teaspoon of baking powder
2 teaspoons of cocoa powder
100 g (4 oz) of caster sugar
100 g (4 oz) of margarine (softened)
2 large eggs
1 tablespoon of milk
1 x 58 g Mars bar (cut into 8 slices, including ends)
8 cupcake cases

Set the oven to gas mark 4/180°C/350°F/Aga baking oven.

Blend the flour, baking powder, cocoa powder, sugar and margarine together until they form a breadcrumb texture.

Add the eggs and milk and process to a soft texture – add a little more milk if necessary.

Put the cases into a patty tin with at least 8 holes and drop one dessertspoon of the cake mixture into each.

Add a slice of Mars and top with the remaining cake mixture.

Bake in the preheated oven for 15-20 minutes or until firm to the touch.

Cool on a wire tray.

Lazy Cook Tips

To mix by hand, cream the margarine and sugar until light and fluffy.

Whisk the eggs together and fold in the remaining ingredients, except the Mars bar.

Follow the recipe to make up for baking. I first tested these on our little friend James. The verdict: 'Absolutely delicious!'

GINGERBREAD BISCUITS & SHAPES

100 g (4 oz) of softened margarine
225 g (8 oz) of self-raising flour
100 g (4 oz) of demerara sugar
1 teaspoon of ground ginger
1 dessertspoon of black treacle
1 dessertspoon of golden syrup
1 dessertspoon of marmalade

Set the oven to gas mark 4/180°C/350°F/Aga baking oven.

Combine the flour, sugar and ginger in a food processor and blend for a few seconds. Add all remaining ingredients and process into a ball of paste.

TO MAKE BY HAND:

Melt the margarine in a saucepan, add all the remaining ingredients and stir together to a paste. Follow the recipe to shape and bake.

TO MAKE INTO BISCUITS:

Spoon generous teaspoons of the mixture onto a lightly oiled baking tray and flatten with a damp fork before baking.

TO MAKE INTO SHAPES:

Roll the paste onto a lightly floured board or table to 5 mm (¼ inch) thickness and cut into shapes. Place on a lightly oiled baking tray and bake for 15-20 minutes or until golden. Remove from the oven and cool on a wire rack. Store in an airtight tin.

LAZY COOK TIPS

Cut into shapes to fit the occasion, i.e. for a bonfire or children's party cut into gingerbread boy and girl shapes.

At Christmas, cut into star shapes, and before baking, pierce with a skewer to make a hole. Thread through with a ribbon and hang on the tree as a festive home-made decoration.

HONEY OAT BISCUITS

*This is the simplest of biscuits to make using good healthy ingredients —
perfect to add to a lunchbox.*

Makes 16
50 g (2 oz) of margarine
75 g (3 oz) of porridge oats
75 g (3 oz) of plain flour
1 generous tablespoon of runny honey
2 tablespoons of milk

QUICK
FIX

Set the oven to gas mark 4/180°C/350°F/Aga baking oven.

Melt the margarine in a pan, add all the remaining ingredients and stir to a
sticky paste.

Put generous teaspoons of the mixture onto a lightly oiled baking tray and
flatten with a damp fork before baking in the preheated oven for 15-20
minutes or until they begin to brown.

Cool on a wire tray and store in an airtight tin.

CRANBERRY & CHOCOLATE ROCKS

Makes 12

225 g (8 oz) of plain flour

1 heaped teaspoon of baking powder

50 g (2 oz) of demerara sugar

40 g (1½ oz) of lard (cut into small pieces)

40 g (1½ oz) of margarine (cut into small pieces)

75 g (3 oz) of dried cranberries

25 g (1 oz) of ready-grated chocolate

1 egg

2 tablespoons of milk

Set the oven to gas mark 4/180°C/350°F/Aga baking oven.

Process the flour, baking powder, sugar and fats to a pastry crumb texture. Add the cranberries, chocolate and egg to the mixture. Pour the milk in (through the funnel) and process until a stiff moist dough is formed.

Pile 12 uneven heaps of the mixture onto a lightly oiled baking tray (this can be done using 2 forks or with fingers) and bake in the preheated oven for 20-30 minutes. Remove from oven and put onto a wire tray to cool.

LAZY COOK TIPS

If you are making these with children, you may prefer to mix the ingredients by hand as follows:

Put the flour and baking powder into a bowl and mix together.

Add the lard and margarine and, using your fingertips, rub them into the flour, then stir in the sugar, cranberries and chocolate.

Whisk the egg and milk together before pouring into the bowl.

Work the ingredients together to make a stiff, moist dough using a wooden spoon or fingers – follow the instructions for shaping and baking as above.

DATE & OAT CHOCOLATE BLOCKS

Another recipe to involve the children, who will have great fun making and eating these.

Makes 25

50 g (2 oz) of porridge oats (browned)
175 g (6 oz) of unsalted butter or margarine
25 g (1 oz) of cocoa powder
2 tablespoons of golden syrup
175 g (6 oz) of digestive biscuits (crushed)
175 g (6 oz) of stoned dates (each cut into 3 pieces)
100 g (4 oz) of chocolate (dark or milk)

Use a strip of foil to line the base and ends of a 20 cm (8 inch) square baking tin and butter lightly.

Brown the oats under a grill or in the roasting oven of an Aga.

Melt the butter in a pan, stir in the cocoa powder and syrup before adding the biscuits, oats and dates and stir together.

Pack into the prepared tin and press down firmly. Melt the chocolate and spread evenly on top.

When cold, remove from the tin and cut into wedges. Store in an airtight tin or container.

LAZY COOK TIPS

The biscuits can be crushed in a food processor or by breaking them into pieces, putting them in a polythene bag and rolling with a rolling pin.

CHOCOLATE WHOLEMEAL BISCUITS

Makes 30-35

175 g (6 oz) of wholemeal flour
25 g (1 oz) of plain white flour
1 heaped teaspoon of baking powder
25 g (1 oz) of porridge oats
75 g (3 oz) of demerara sugar
50 g (2 oz) of ready-grated chocolate
100 g (4 oz) of margarine
100 ml (4 fl oz) of milk
100 g (4 oz) of melted chocolate (dark or milk, optional)

Set oven to gas mark 4/180°C/350°F/Aga baking oven. Grease a large baking tray.

Put the flour, baking powder, oats, sugar, grated chocolate and margarine (cut into pieces) into a food processor and blend for a few seconds.

Pour in the milk and continue processing until a paste is formed.

Dollop generous teaspoons of the paste onto the prepared baking tray and flatten each with a wet fork. Bake in the preheated oven for 15-20 minutes. Cool on a wire tray. To make a richer biscuit, spread the base of each cooked biscuit with melted chocolate and when set hard store the biscuits in an airtight container.

TO MAKE BY HAND:

Melt the margarine in a saucepan, add all the remaining ingredients except the optional melted chocolate and stir together to a paste. Follow the recipe to shape and bake.

LAZY COOK TIPS

Ready-grated chocolate is an essential ingredient in my store cupboard and saves time – you don't have to grate it yourself. I recommend the superior quality of Charbonnel et Walker, Chocolat Charbonnel.

PICNIC SLICES

A yummy tray bake from the Seventies.

Makes 24
200 g bar of Bourneville chocolate
50 g (2 oz) of unsalted butter (softened)
50 g (2 oz) of caster sugar
100 g (4 oz) of desiccated coconut
50 g (2 oz) of glacé cherries
50 g (2 oz) of sultanas
1 large egg

Set the oven to gas mark 4/180°C/350°F/Aga baking oven.

Melt the chocolate and spread it over the base of a lightly buttered baking tin (Swiss roll type). Leave to set.

In a food processor, mix together the sugar and coconut for a few seconds.

Add all the remaining ingredients.

Evenly spread the mixture over the set chocolate and bake in the preheated oven for 25-30 minutes.

When cold, mark into squares and remove – use a palette knife to ease them from the tray. Store in an airtight tin.

LAZY COOK TIPS

When the tin is lined with the melted chocolate, it can be put into a fridge to speed up the hardening process.

Children will enjoy mixing these ingredients in a bowl. Cut up the cherries but leave the sultanas whole.

Lazy Cook Notes

EATING WELL WHEN FUNDS ARE SHORT

It is my experience that when strapped for cash it is the food budget that suffers first. Remember, a healthy diet is a well-balanced diet. Below I give a few simple tips on keeping yourself and your family, fed and healthy, whilst keeping sane!

Shop once a week and always with a shopping list. During the coming week, jot down the meals your family enjoys. We allow time to plan a holiday, why not plan our daily diet?

Think 'big'. With the possible exception of fish, most meat or poultry will keep fresh in a fridge for a few days before cooking (note the use by dates). Avoid buying individual portions of meat, poultry or fish. Rather buy a joint, a whole chicken or a fillet of fish, which will last for several meals. Remember that in most cases allowing cooked ingredients to rest for a while in a fridge will enrich the flavour.

Cut down, not out. 'Hello Hard Times, Goodbye Obesity' is my motto. This is the perfect time to eat less and feel better for it.

Waste nothing. I could put my weekly food waste into a brown paper bag. Those few tablespoons of gravy, vegetable stock or leftover sauces will transform a few ingredients into a tasty meal in minutes. Have a regular 'fridge tidy' putting all edible leftover bits together to make a soup or a bake topped with a few shavings of cheese.

Remember the 3 Ps – Planning, Preparation, Presentation. Follow these rules and your meals will look good and taste good. Nothing will be left on the plate, giving you a feeling of great satisfaction

Keep a well-stocked store cupboard of ingredients you regularly use. There is a huge range of ready-prepared ingredients available which will save on time and energy in the preparation of meals. I recommend ready-baked pastry cases, ready-rolled puff pastry and oven chips – the best thing since sliced bread!

Bags of short grain brown rice from your nearest health food shop are very useful, as are tins of chopped tomatoes and tubes or small jars of tomato purée (keep these in a fridge once opened).

Other staples to keep stock of are mustards and sauces, dried herbs, jars of sun-dried tomatoes and artichoke hearts in oil, capers, cocktail onions and olives. Stock up with your favourite flavours and they will transform seemingly ordinary ingredients into a delicious meal in minutes.

Store Cupboard Essentials

The choice of store cupboard is a personal one, but in addition to the basics, dairy and perishables, the following is a list of ingredients I find it useful to keep stock of. Many of these items are used in the recipes in this book and will also, I trust, assist your conversion to Lazy Cooking. Personally, without some of these ingredients I panic. They enable me to put a meal together quickly if I run out of food before the next weekly shop, or if at short notice I have unexpected extra mouths to feed.

IN THE FREEZER

Baking
Bread and rolls
Ready-rolled puff pastry

Fish/Meat
A whole chicken or small joint of meat
Minced meat (450g/1 lb) – beef, lamb, pork or veal
Sausages
White fish fillets

Miscellaneous
Bags of home-made stock
Mixed berries
Vanilla ice cream

Vegetables
Broad beans
Oven chips
Peas
Spinach
Sweetcorn

IN THE STORE CUPBOARD/LARDER

Baking
Breadcrumbs (dried)
Bread flour (white and wholemeal)
Dried active yeast for hand-baking
Dried fruit (a selection including whole apricots and pitted prunes)
Ready-baked pastry cases (savoury and sweet)
Ready-grated chocolate (Charbonnel et Walker)
Spices and whole nutmegs

Flavourings
Gravy browning
Marmite
Mushroom ketchup
Mustards (a variety including wholegrain and Dijon)
Pickles and chutneys, piccalilli
Sun-dried tomato paste and purée
Tapenade (green olive paste)
Vinegars (balsamic, cider, wine)
Worcestershire sauce

Jams/Jellies
Runny honey
Lemon curd
Marmalade
Mincemeat
Redcurrant and mint jelly
A selection of jams

Miscellaneous
Artichoke hearts in oil
Bacon slices (back or streaky — with long use-by date)
Blackcurrants in syrup
A selection of dried herbs
Olives — pitted black with soft crinkled skins (from Provence or Spain)

Rice, pasta and noodles (a selection)
Stock cubes (fish, meat, vegetable)
Sun-dried tomatoes (jars in oil)
Sun-dried tomatoes (dried, in packets)

Oils
Olive and sunflower oils

Tins
Baked Beans
Chopped tomatoes (all sizes)
Lentils
Sardines in oil
Soups (condensed) — chicken and mushroom
Sweetcorn

OVEN TEMPERATURES

Ovens can vary considerably so the temperatures given below and those quoted in the recipes should be treated as a guide and adjusted according to your own cooker. Aga owners should refer to their instruction manual.

Temperature	Gas Mark	Celsius/Fahrenheit	Fan
Slow	1	110°/225°	80°
Warm	2	150°/300°	130°
Moderate/simmering	3	160°/325°	140°
Baking	4	180°/350°	160°
Roasting	6	200°/400°	180°
High roasting	7	220°/425°	200°

INDEX